FROMMER'S
WALKING TOURS
CHICAGO

BY
MICHAEL UHL

PRENTICE HALL TRAVEL

NEW YORK • LONDON • TORONTO • SYDNEY
TOKYO • SINGAPORE

FROMMER BOOKS

Published by Prentice Hall Reference
15 Columbus Circle
New York, NY 10023

Copyright © 1994 by Simon & Schuster, Inc.

PRENTICE HALL is a registered trademark and colophon is a trademark of Prentice-Hall, Inc.

Library of Congress Cataloging-in-Publication Data

Uhl, Michael.
    Frommer's Walking Tours: Chicago / by Michael Uhl.
        p.   c.m.
    Includes index.
    ISBN 0-671-88503-0 : $12.00
    1. Chicago (Ill.)—Tours. 2. Walking—Illinois—Chicago—
    Guidebooks.
    I. Title. II. Series.
    F548.18.U37   1994   94-6480
    917.73'110443—dc20   CIP

Design by Robert Bull Design
Maps by Ortelius Design

FROMMER'S EDITORIAL STAFF

Editorial Director: Marilyn Wood
Editor-in-Chief: Leanne Coupe
Executive Editor: Alice Fellows
Senior Editor: Lisa Renaud
Editors: Charlotte Allstrom, Margaret Bowen, Thomas F. Hirsch, Peter
    Katucki, Theodore Stavrou, Alice Thompson
Assistant Editors: Douglas Stallings, Ian Wilker
Production Supervisor: Brian Bondarchuk
Digital Cartographers: John Decamillis, Devorah Wilkenfeid

SPECIAL SALES

Bulk purchases of Frommer's Travel Guides are available at special discounts. The publishers are happy to custom-make publications for corporate clients who wish to use them as premiums or sales promotions. We can excerpt the contents, provide covers with corporate imprints, or create books to meet specific needs. For more information, write to Special Sales, Prentice Hall Travel, Paramount Communications Building, 15 Columbus Circle, New York, NY 10023.

Manufactured in the United States of America

CONTENTS

LIST OF MAPS

A SAFETY ADVISORY

Whenever you're traveling in an unfamiliar city or country, stay alert. Be aware of your immediate surroundings. Wear a moneybelt and keep a close eye on your possessions. Be particularly careful with cameras, purses, and wallets, all favorite targets of thieves and pickpockets.

INVITATION TO THE READERS

In researching this book, I have come across many wonderful sights, shops, and restaurants, the best of which I have included here. I'm sure that many of you will also discover appealing places as you explore Chicago. Please don't keep them to yourself. Share your experiences, especially if you want to bring to my attention information that has changed since this book was researched. You can address your letters to:

Michael Uhl
Frommer's Walking Tours: Chicago
Prentice Hall Travel
15 Columbus Circle
New York, NY 10023

Introducing Chicago

There are really only two *big* cities in America: New York and Chicago. *Big* cities require tall buildings, dense downtown areas, streetlife, and sprawling neighborhoods radiating out from the center—neighborhoods that project an urban, not a suburban, flavor. As big cities go in the United States, New York City is number one and Chicago is number two. Chicago has never suggested it might surpass the great metropolis of the East. Indeed, Chicago has long dubbed itself the Second City. But to be second to New York in financial clout, commerce, printing, advertising, theater, the arts, and museums—not to mention in the Old World flavor of its ethnic neighborhoods—requires more than empty braggadocio. You've got to have something to show for yourself. The boosters here—who gave Chicago another of its many nicknames, the Windy City—aren't just blowing hot air when they boast about the quality of life in the "City by the Lake."

Civic pride runs high in Chicago; it always has. During all those years when the rest of the world could only imagine Chicago as a haven for crooks and corrupt politicians, as a "jungle" of slaughterhouses and meatpackers, as a dismal "city of big shoulders," Chicagoans have gone about their worldly affairs—one of which involved building the most architecturally sophisticated city in the world. In a head-on race with New York, architectural innovation against architectural innovation, Chicago wins hands down.

For years, to attract visitors other than the loyal provincials from surrounding states who came into town periodically for a dose of big-city life, Chicagoans rolled up their sleeves and built the most successful convention trade in the country. But for the "destination" travelers from a wider world who'd think nothing of hopping from coast to coast for a long getaway weekend, Chicago was just a stopover at O'Hare, a place where you changed planes. Chicago? A destination? Gimme a break!

Happily, that misconception is rapidly disappearing. More and more travelers, international and domestic, are being drawn to Chicago every year, and not just for business. They're coming to have a good time. Bed for bed, you'd be hard pressed to find a city with a better infrastructure of fine hotels. And you don't have to be rich to stay in one—at least if you come on the weekends, when rates are often slashed as much as 50%, and can include a package of amenities from breakfast and free parking to tickets for a local show. As for the food, Chicago's reputation as a place where you'd better stick to steaks and chops is long gone. You still might not be able to find better steaks, chops, and ribs anywhere else in America, but in modern culinary terms, this town has grown up, and its restaurants can go toe to toe with the best of them . . . anywhere!

THE ART OF A GOOD "CONSTITUTIONAL"

One of the great pleasures of urban living is the cultivated habit of taking a walk. It's a very civilized avocation, invigorating to both body and spirit. In the country, you hike vigorously and commune with nature; in the city, you shift into cruising gear, a very nonathletic natural gait that allows for alternating moods of meditation and observation. A walking tour, of course, is a more purposeful form of the urban stroll, an itinerary aimed at following the footsteps of history in a particular neighborhood, or, as is often the case in Chicago, studying up close the city's remarkable wonders of architecture or public art.

The walking tours presented in this guide concentrate primarily on Chicago's downtown core, and—with the exceptions of Oak Park and Hyde Park—on those older neighborhoods within its immediate periphery. You can easily walk to the beginning of most tours from virtually any downtown hotel, though advice on the most convenient form of public transportation accompanies each itinerary.

CHICAGO'S ROOTS

The city you see before you has its modern roots in the early 19th century; Chicago is a relatively recent phenomenon, even in the context of the historical youth of the United States. Indeed, use of the word "phenomenon" when referring to Chicago is more than hyperbole. In 1840, Chicago had a population of barely 5,000; by 1880 the number of its inhabitants had increased a hundred-fold, totaling 500,000. Chicago's growth was a yardstick against which the American Republic could measure the realization of its Manifest Destiny, the inexorable spread of its authority and settlements from coast to coast.

The significance of the geographical locale that would in time evolve into the city of Chicago was known to European explorers as early as 1673. In that year, Marquette and Jolliet, who labored assiduously to expand the French Empire throughout North America, had been shown by their Native American allies the portage trail between two nearby but disconnected rivers linking ancient trade routes of the Mississippi Valley to those along Lake Michigan and beyond, creating in effect an inland waterway between the Atlantic Ocean and the Gulf of Mexico. Chicago lay at the perfect intersection between those two water routes, at the mouth of the river on the eastern end of that portage which emptied into Lake Michigan.

But it was only in 1803, two decades after the War of Independence ended, that the fledgling Republic, having finally wrested the Northwest Territory from the grip of remaining British forces, established its military presence with a frontier fort on the site where the Michigan Avenue Bridge today crosses the Chicago River. But tensions between Native Americans and white settlers grew; Fort Dearborn was destroyed, and its inhabitants were massacred during a raid in 1812. Four years later, the fort was rebuilt, and only in 1833, with a population of slightly more than 300 inhabitants, was the town of Chicago officially incorporated.

What began as a transportation and shipping hub for pioneers and materials being carried westward to the plains states and beyond in exchange for the grain and livestock returned to the east soon developed into a major industrial and manufacturing center in its own right. Before continuing east, livestock was concentrated in the Chicago Stockyards, and packed into meat products. Regional deposits of coal and iron ore led to the establishment of steel mills and factories where heavy machinery was produced. But the role of playing national middleman between east and west never ceased to be a major factor in Chicago's economy. It's no coincidence that the mail-order giants of the American retail trade, like Sears, Roebuck & Company and Montgomery Ward, grew up and retained their headquarters in Chicago. For many decades, hardly a single train originating on either coast, or any point in between for that matter, didn't pass through Chicago. With connections like that, it didn't take Chicago long to become the literal hub of industry, manufacturing, commerce, and finance for the entire central core of the country.

THE GREAT FIRE

Who, then, could have anticipated that this vibrant, still rough-and-ready frontier metropolis of the heartland would be nearly struck from the map in two short days by a raging conflagration? Somewhere on the southwest side of the city, where Mrs. O'Leary's fictitious cow was thought to have resided, a fire began on the evening of October 8,

1871. The flames, fed by the acres of wooden homes and roadway planking, quickly spread northward, consuming all of downtown Chicago before leaping the Chicago River and leveling residential neighborhoods as far north as current-day Fullerton Avenue. By October 10, with the help of explosives, the flames moving south were checked, while a rainfall finally quenched the northside fires, ending the long drought that had made tinder of the city's wooden structures just before the flames spread to the grassy plains of the surrounding prairie.

Two hundred and fifty residents lost their lives. Eighteen thousand buildings were reduced to ashes, leaving 90,000 people homeless. Damage was assessed at $200 million. An area covering four square miles, including the business district, was completely destroyed. Two major resources remained unscathed, however, in addition to the city's resilient population. The first, inherently immutable, was Chicago's strategic location; the second, of more immediate significance, was the city's infrastructure of railroads, manufacturing plants, grain warehouses, and lumberyards, which had been miraculously spared. For the most part, these facilities were located on the city's southern rim, beyond the circle of the fire.

With the aid of national and international relief funds, Chicago staged a remarkable comeback. By 1873, the city's downtown business district was already rebuilt. The Great Fire had spurred an unprecedented renaissance in building and architecture. From 1885, when William Le Baron Jenny built the Home Insurance Building, considered the first modern skyscraper, to 1894, 21 buildings between 12 and 16 stories high were erected in downtown Chicago. By 1893, Chicago had recovered sufficiently to host the World's Columbian Exposition, an honor it won over four other contending American cities, including New York.

THE CRADLE OF THE AMERICAN LABOR MOVEMENT

Yankee ingenuity was the driving force behind the initial growth and success of Chicago. The early pioneers had followed the westward migration, leaving ancestral homes in the Northeast where, in many cases, their families had settled during the founding epoch of the Massachusetts theocracy. But the real population explosion in Chicago was the by-product of 19th-century mass immigration from Europe. By 1890, the foreign-born and their children made up three-quarters of Chicago's population. It was these immigrants who made the factories run, who provided the "big shoulders" upon which the great fortunes of Chicago's industrial and merchant princes were made.

Most of the great labor battles in the United States for shorter hours, higher wages, and better working conditions from the 1870s through the 1890s were centered in the mills and manufacturies of Chicago. Two legendary struggles, the Pullman Strike and the issues leading up to the so-called Haymarket Riot, will live forever in the annals of American labor as highwater marks in the workingman's quest for fairness and justice on the job. May Day, as an international day commemorating workers, had its origin with a parade in Chicago on May 1, 1886, calling for the eight-hour work day.

POLITICS, GANGSTERS & RACE

By virtue of its location, Chicago also developed early on into a powerhouse on the national political scene. Between 1860 and 1968, Chicago played host to 14 Republican and 10 Democratic presidential nominating conventions. The first Chicago convention gave the nation one of its most admired leaders, Abraham Lincoln, while the last was witness to the riots between Chicago police and anti-Vietnam War demonstrators, who had come to stage their protest at the Democratic Convention that nominated Hubert Humphrey.

No image of this city is more longstanding, especially beyond our national borders, than that of Chicago as a haven for tommy gun-toting gangsters and their corrupt allies among politicians, judges, cops, and newsmen during the years of Prohibition. While by no means completely false, this image was never more than a caricature, and little trace of those wild days remains apparent in the Chicago of today. It's not that organized crime has disappeared, nor that corruption has been eliminated among politicians, but the problems of Chicago are not those of its mythic, romantic past. Most of Chicago's difficulties today are those that plague every American city: crime, population flight, and declining fiscal resources, especially in the areas of social services, health care, and education. As with other American cities, these problems are often aggravated by the racial tensions between blacks and whites.

Chicago, though, more than most large American cities today, has managed to keep up appearances. The city, especially those areas covered by these walking tours, seems amazingly peaceful and clean—almost polished in places. And Chicagoans themselves retain an élan based on the feeling that their city remains a very livable place. Their view is often shared by visitors who are discovering the city's charms for the first time, or returning to deepen their relationship with this most American of American cities.

The Loop: Chicago Architecture

Start: Sears Tower, 233 South Wacker Drive, at West Adams Street.

Public Transportation: Take the Ravenswood or Evanston lines to the Quincy/Wells station. You can also catch a bus from various downtown locations, including numbers 7, 121, 151, or 156, all of which pass near the Sears Tower.

Finish: Dearborn Station Galleria, 47 West Polk Street.

Time: 2 to 3 hours.

Best Times: Weekends during daylight hours, especially Saturdays, when most buildings are open. Strolling and pausing unhurriedly to really take in the buildings is at its most comfortable when the street and auto traffic are minimal. Weekdays are next best, or even preferable, if you like your cityscapes against a backdrop of human hustle and bustle.

Worst Times: Nights should be avoided for security and because you can't see well enough to appreciate the architectural details that are most visible in daylight.

There are two poles to downtown Chicago, north and south of the Chicago River. The old downtown to the south is known as the Loop, so called because many of its blocks lie within a large area enclosed by a system of elevated train tracks. Contained in the Loop and its immediate environs are the city's principal financial, cultural, and governmental centers. Across the Michigan Avenue Bridge, running north along the Magnificent Mile is the high-rent district of downtown Chicago, with the city's newest and most luxurious hotels, upscale vertical malls, and specialty shops, and its most desirable commercial office space (see Walking Tour 5, "The Magnificent Mile"). Still, when city residents mention "downtown," it is likely that they have in mind this densely packed canyon of buildings in the Loop, whose most venerable structures rose in a burst of civic reconstruction immediately following the Great Fire of 1871.

Chicago owes its present-day reputation as an architectural mecca to this tragic conflagration that virtually leveled the town and presented it with the necessity of rebuilding itself anew. Since that time, Chicago has been a haven to architects of many visions, who over time have transformed the Loop into an open-air showroom of architectural style and innovation: From the engineering of the first skyscrapers to the sprawling, purely functional emporia where Chicago's merchant princes displayed their acres of commodities, to the fanciful excesses of ornamentation and design associated early on with Sullivan and Wright, and more recently, with Helmut Jahn and Philip Johnson, for whom the ideals of beauty and utility were inseparable.

Our walk proceeds from the south end of Wacker Drive, follows the river as it bends toward Lake Michigan, then plunges south once again into the core of the Loop, as we zig-zag block by block among the neighborhood's most representative architectural oddities and treasures.

Begin at the:

1. **Sears Tower,** at 1,454 feet, currently the world's tallest building. When the Sears company chose this site for its new corporate headquarters, the decision was controversial. Many city planners saw the Loop as a neighborhood in decline. While Sears itself has since relocated its offices, the mere presence of the giant skyscraper since its completion in 1974 has stimulated the construction of more than 100 new buildings in Chicago's traditional downtown area.

   The 110-story mega-tower was built to accommodate 16,500 office workers, 5,000 of whom, originally, were Sears' employees. The Sears Tower's foundation rests on 114 caissons of concrete and steel sunk to bedrock 65 feet below the building's three sub-basements. Architecturally, the building is considered more a triumph of engineering than design. But seen from a distance, it is incontestable that the Sears Tower has a unique and imposing profile that dominates the Chicago skyline from surrounding neighborhoods along practically every point on the compass.

A ride to the building's observation decks (one on the 100th floor, the other on the 103rd floor) is a popular attraction for visitors and residents alike, especially school-age children on field trips. The ascent usually requires a wait of 15 minutes. While you're walking toward the elevators, note the Calder wall sculpture with movable parts installed in the lobby.

When you leave the Sears Tower, continue walking north on:

2. Wacker Drive. The many modern buildings lining the drive may or may not appeal to you, but few cities offer a downtown stroll as pleasant as this one. The proximity of the river and the width of the roadway here create an atmosphere of openness, as if you were at the very bottom of the urban canyon, rather than among the narrow mule paths of the Loop's interior streets.

Wacker Drive is named for Charles Wacker, a civic-minded brewer and a director of the World's Columbian Exposition of 1893, who lobbied tirelessly for a plan to replace the old South Water Street Market, once the principal feature along the riverbank, with this double-leveled thoroughfare which bears his name.

As you walk north you will see on your left the "Merc," the Chicago Mercantile Exchange Center at number 31 south, housing one of the great trading chambers for Midwestern commodities. The Civic Opera Building stands at number 20 north (street addresses change from south to north when you cross Madison Street). It was built by Samuel Insull, the utility magnate, to house a 3,500-seat opera house and a 900-seat theater in an office building where rents would be used to subsidize the arts. The Grand Foyer of the opera house, with its 40-foot-high ceiling, is worth a peek, when the building is open.

Continue north and follow Wacker Drive as it bends to the east. At the midpoint of that bend is:

3. 333 West Wacker Drive. The facade of this building suggests a massive convex, green-tinted, multipaned looking glass—or a magnified fly's eye, highly stylized.

The building's curved exterior accompanies the curve in the Chicago River, and it's from the middle of the river that the magic reflections cast by this glassy cladding are best observed. How do you stand in the middle of the river? On a boat, ideally an architectural river tour organized by the **Chicago Architecture Foundation** (tel. 922-TOUR). As the boat approaches 333 West Wacker from either direction, a grand visual pageant unfolds upon the building's mirrored surface where the cityscape and skyline to your rear are projected in an unbroken, film-like continuum.

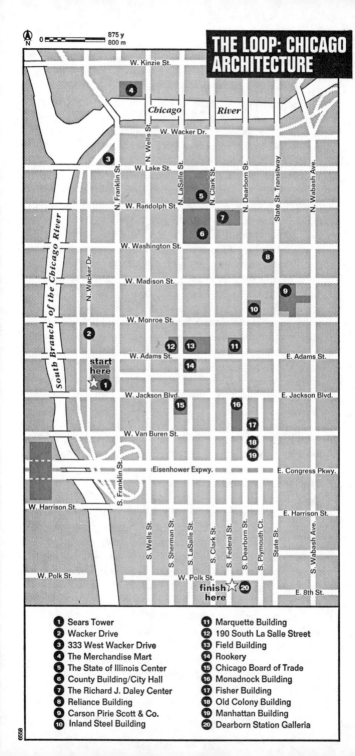

THE LOOP: CHICAGO ARCHITECTURE

1. Sears Tower
2. Wacker Drive
3. 333 West Wacker Drive
4. The Merchandise Mart
5. The State of Illinois Center
6. County Building/City Hall
7. The Richard J. Daley Center
8. Reliance Building
9. Carson Pirie Scott & Co.
10. Inland Steel Building
11. Marquette Building
12. 190 South La Salle Street
13. Field Building
14. Rookery
15. Chicago Board of Trade
16. Monadnock Building
17. Fisher Building
18. Old Colony Building
19. Manhattan Building
20. Dearborn Station Galleria

Lacking a boat to stand on in mid-river, walk out on the Franklin Avenue Bridge, a stationary vantage point from which you can witness something of the same hypnotic effect.

The building's winning design is all the more remarkable when you consider that this 36-story tower had to be squeezed onto a rather awkward plot of triangular real estate that was previously thought suitable only for a parking lot.

Directly across the river is:

4. The Merchandise Mart. Touted as the world's largest commercial building, containing some 4.1 million square feet of rentable space, the Mart is a Chicago landmark as much for its place in the saga of American merchandising as for its hulking institutional presence. The building went up in the late 1920s, and where a few sparse elements of design grace its asylum-like facade, they are discreetly deco in their intention. Built by Marshall Field as a wholesale emporium, the Mart was purchased by Joseph P. Kennedy (JFK's dad) in 1945, and is still owned and operated by the Kennedy family, and today serves as a showcase for dealers of furniture and furnishings. Perched atop a line of pillars running the length of the building along the river pier are oversized busts of the icons of American merchandising, including Marshall Field, Edward Filene, George Huntington Hartford (A&P), Julius Rosenwald (Sears), John N. Wanamaker, and Aaron Montgomery Ward.

Keep walking east along Wacker Drive and turn right onto La Salle Street, continuing south two blocks to Randolph Street. Now turn left (east) on Randolph Street and walk a half block; you will be standing before:

5. The State of Illinois Center. This post-modern cascade of glass and steel is, depending on your point of view, the masterwork or folly of the celebrated contemporary architect Helmut Jahn. Within the building's million-plus-square-foot interior, the State of Illinois shelters the Chicago branches of its many-tiered bureaucracy—some 50 agencies in all, from the tourist authority to the Motor Vehicle Bureau. On every floor, the transparent glass walls that enclose the offices allow the public to observe their tax dollars at work.

To some, the bowl-shaped State of Illinois Center looks like a stadium from the outside. Apart from the obvious patriotic allusions, the peculiar hues of blue, silver, and salmon visible in the building's glass-and-steel sheathing suggest the gaudy colors of the De Sotos and Edsels manufactured by Detroit's automotive industry in the 1950s.

One theme said to underlie the architect's design is a symbolic reference to "open government," with its implied invitation for the public to come in and feel welcome. But the vast rotunda that greets you on entering here, with its several levels of shops and galleries, doesn't require any subliminal manipulation to entice the public. The appeal of this vast mall-like atrium, which rises the full 17 floors of the building, is self-evident, making it an obvious choice for a bit of light browsing among the many retail stalls, for sitting over a cup of coffee and a danish at some counter or café, or for a comfort stop in that vanishing urban institution, the public bathroom, which the state in its wisdom has seen fit to locate here on the basement level. On the plaza facing Randolph Street stands a public sculpture by Dubuffet, to which we will return in Walking Tour 11, "The Loop Sculpture Tour."

Now cross Randolph Street, and continue south along Clark Street. The squat, many-columned twin structure occupying the block encompassed by Clark, Randolph, La Salle and Washington streets is the combined:

6. County Building/City Hall. Actually, City Hall fronts La Salle Street, and the County Building, the older and more classical in appearance of the two government centers, faces Clark Street, where you should now be standing. Typically beaux arts in its classical appointments, as were many of the public edifices erected in the early years of this century, the County Building was designed in part by one of Chicago's legendary architectural firms, Holabird and Roche. Especially worthy of note are the Corinthian columns gracing the facade; at a height of 75 feet, they're still the largest columns constructed in the city of Chicago. The massive capitals topping each column are themselves the height of a single floor, and, as purely decorative additions, are supported by caissons 10 feet in diameter.

Across Clark Street and fronting a broad plaza along Washington Street, is:

7. The Richard J. Daley Center, named for the late mayor and longtime czar of Cook County politics. You can be excused for imagining that this tall and boxy monolith is the work of the still-reigning patron saint of Chicago architecture, the late Ludwig Mies van der Rohe. It is not. The building copies his idiom, but is merely a "wannabe." The singular characteristic of the Daley Center, completed in 1965, is that, despite its height of 648 feet, the building has only 31 stories. It dwarfs its neighbor, the Madison Building, across Washington Street on the corner at Dearborn, which squeezes 38 stories into a height just under 500 feet.

Many architectural critics pour on the sugary superlatives when contemplating the starkness and simplicity of this structure and others like it, but I personally find it distasteful, an affirmation of the Puritan streak in the American psyche.

The number one tourist photo-op in all Chicago is to stand posed before the untitled Picasso sculpture, in residence on Daley Plaza since 1966.

Cross Washington Street, turn left, and walk two blocks east, turning south onto State Street. At 32 North State Street is the entrance to the:

8. Reliance Building. A relic of the early days of the First Chicago School of Architecture, the Reliance Building is seen today as a prototype of the modern skyscraper, whose height was made possible by the simultaneous development of high-speed elevators and steel framing. The building's foundation and base were constructed in 1891, the work of John Wellborn Root, who died that year before the building could be completed. Root's partner, Daniel Burnham, who would later be remembered as the chief architect of the 1893 World's Columbian Exposition and as the creator of the Chicago Plan (a sweeping blueprint, only partially implemented, for the total revamping of the city's streets, parks, and plazas) finally finished the Reliance Building in 1895 with the help of a new designer, Charles Atwood. Atwood is credited with the decision to employ the use of so much glass on the terra-cotta facade, which gives the building its modern appearance, and with the design of what would later be known as the Chicago Window, a large central pane of glass, flanked by two smaller double-hung windows used for ventilation.

The next stop showcases the work of Louis Henri Sullivan, who embodied the great romantic spirit of Chicago architecture, a man whose lyrical vision was a counterpoint to the pure utilitarianism of his many contemporaries. Sullivan also significantly influenced Frank Lloyd Wright, who apprenticed in his firm. Cross the State Street Mall, and continue to the southeast corner of East Madison Street. There, at 1 South State Street, stands the magnificent facade of:

9. Carson Pirie Scott & Co. This building still houses one of Chicago's oldest department stores, which retains its hint of elegance from bygone days. In designing a home for this vast merchandising enterprise, Sullivan was required to consider the need for horizontal and open interior spaces. Two of Sullivan's design features, however, prevented the building from imitating the shoebox and warehouse style that typified the other State Street department stores of that period. Sullivan placed the entrance at the corner of the building, above which rises a multistoried tower that combines the visual and technical effects of a skyscraper. And finally, the poet in Sullivan would not allow the building to stand unadorned. The ornate metalwork, particularly that above the entrance, suggests what one critic termed "a kind of poetic representation of nature capable of offsetting the materialist culture of an industrialized modern city."

Recross State Street and continue west down Madison Street to Dearborn Street. Notice the Chicago Building on the corner, just across from Carson Pirie Scott at 7 West Madison. The building dates from 1904, and makes full use of the Chicago window motif on the facades of its exterior walls. Notice too how the original cornice runs unbroken along the top of the roofline, an unusual feature among Chicago buildings of this vintage, which were so often subjected to renovation and alteration. Turn left on Dearborn Street and continue south along the east side of the street for one block. On the corner at 30 West Monroe Street is the:

10. Inland Steel Building. Construction of Inland Steel was completed in 1958, and the building boasts many firsts for Chicago in its engineering and design. For example, all the building's "mechanicals"—elevators and risers for plumbing, heating, and ventilation—are in the eastern tower. The building also shows off the advances in steel manufacturing that had taken place during World War II, not only in its framework and shimmering stainless steel cladding, but also with its invisible supports, steel pilings driven through 85 feet of swampy Loop soil into the Chicago bedrock. Inland Steel was the first air-conditioned building in Chicago, the first to double-glaze its windows, and the first to offer indoor parking below street level. Finally, the soft glimmer of Inland Steel's floor-to-ceiling emerald-green windows creates an effect of post-modern eclecticism that marks the building as seemingly contemporary because it was once so ahead of its time.

Across Dearborn Street the sunken plaza around the giant First National Bank of Chicago Building is a favorite lunchtime gathering spot for those who work in the Loop. A fountain and another of Chicago's well-known public sculptures, *The Four Seasons* by Marc Chagall, also grace this outdoor sanctuary. Walking down the plaza side of Dearborn Street, continue south one block to Adams Street.

REFUELING STOP An ideal spot for a midday pick-me-up and a light snack is the barroom at **Berghoff's** (tel. 427-3170), one block east (toward State Street) at 17 West Adams Street. Beer on tap, along with many other alcoholic and non-alcoholic beverages, wursts, and sandwiches are the typical fare served in the rathskeller-style tavern at Berghoff's; for a full meal from the tasty lunch or dinner menus, moderately priced and quickly served, you will have to be seated in the restaurant itself, a Chicago landmark for more than 90 years. Open Monday to Thursday from 11am to 9:30pm, Friday and Saturday from 11am to 10pm.

Now retrace your steps west along Adams Street and cross to the northwest corner of its intersection with Dearborn, where the tour continues at 104 South Dearborn Street, the:

11. Marquette Building. There is considerable lore—historical and architectural—associated with this early example of the commercial Chicago high-rise. Its name honors the Jesuit explorer Jacques Marquette, whose 1675 journal contains the first descriptions by a European of the site that would one day become the city of Chicago. One of the building's original owners had translated Marquette's journal, and not only gave the priest's name to the edifice, but memorialized the famous expedition undertaken by Marquette and his companion Louis Jolliet in a series of relief sculptures over the building's main portal and above the elevators, and with elaborate scenes in mosaic designed by the Tiffany Glass Company and installed throughout the marble-trimmed lobby.

Architecturally, the Marquette Building has undergone several major transformations over the years. A sixth bay was added on the west side in 1905, and a 17th floor in 1950. A more abstract transformation concerning the Marquette was suggested by Mies van der Rohe when contemplating the design of the complex of buildings across Adams Street, flanking both sides of Dearborn, and known as the Chicago Federal Center. Mies saw the Marquette as the "fourth wall" of his three-cornered complex, and used this theme as a point of departure for his update of the Chicago commercial style, and the geographical point where the First and Second Schools of Chicago Architecture were to meet. In the spacious public plaza at the center of this constellation stands the vermillion-colored stabile *Flamingo,* designed by Alexander Calder.

Follow Adams Street two blocks west again to La Salle Street. At this intersection, on diagonally opposite corners, are two of the most impressive buildings in all of Chicago, buildings that must be entered to be fully appreciated. First, on the northwest corner of La Salle and Adams, is a building known simply as:

12. 190 South La Salle Street. This building is the only work in Chicago by Philip Johnson, an early acolyte of Walter Gropius, the Bauhaus grandmeister himself. Gropius was a refugee from Nazi Germany who traded his career in practical architecture for a teaching position at Harvard, where Johnson was his pupil. But nothing could be further from the rigid functionalism of the early Bauhaus School than the Gothic splendor of this building's lobby under its barrel-vaulted arch and goldleaf ceiling that would rival the central naves of many great European cathedrals in its grandeur and scale. An entrance to the building on Adams Street leads to a small side "chapel" off the main lobby; on the far wall opposite this entrance hangs an elegant tapestry depicting the original layout of Daniel Burnham's "Chicago Plan." And at the north end of the enormous main lobby itself, otherwise completely empty except for an unobtrusive and slab-like security desk at the south end, is a giant wooden sculpture that suggests some kind of mill-work machinery from the Middle Ages.

The exterior of Johnson's 44-story tower is equally impressive. The building's overall design was inspired by John Wellborn Root's Masonic Temple, long since demolished. There are also echoes in the arched windows and doors of Root's Rookery across the way (see Stop 14, below). And while the simple and repetitive detail work of 190 South La Salle Street's exterior walls is attractive in itself, the top of the building is pure fantasy, in the form of a many-gabled cottage, giving the building an unexpected air of country-lane domesticity when it is taken in as a whole.

Before we continue, look up at the massive limestone building directly across La Salle Street from where we were just standing at 190 South La Salle Street. It is the old:

13. Field Building. Commissioned by Marshall Field, this was the last building to be constructed in the Loop between 1934 and 1955, when the combination of the Great Depression and World War II forestalled all construction on this scale. The Field Building itself stands on the site formerly occupied by the Home Insurance Building (1885), the work of William Le Baron Jenny, which some students of architecture believe to have been the first skyscraper ever.

Now cross La Salle Street, walking toward the old Field Building, and then cross Adams Street and walk to number 209 South La Salle Street, the legendary:

14. Rookery. Of the more than two dozen buildings constructed in the Loop by the firm of Burnham and Root in the final two decades of the 19th century, only the Rookery—built between 1885 and 1888—remains. The name "rookery" memorializes a long-demolished city hall building once located across the street, the former roost of many pigeons and politicians. There is no finer relic of Old Chicago in the city today. To begin with, the Rookery's rough granite base and many turrets were almost certainly influenced by the heavy Romanesque style of H. R. Richardson, whose work—with the exception of Glessner House in the historic Prairie Avenue District—has completely disappeared from Chicago.

Furthermore, all the buildings of any dimension raised during this period benefitted from numerous advances in engineering and materials spurred forward by a heightened concern for fireproofing and a need to concentrate growth in an area of the city where real estate was both limited and increasingly in high demand. The Rookery, in this sense, represents a transition in Chicago architecture, combining thick load-bearing masonry walls at its base with innovative iron framing on the upper stories, which, with the introduction of plate glass, allowed for larger windows and therefore more light and better ventilation.

There are many eye-catching details that make the Rookery one of the standout attractions on this tour. The building's exterior is itself the product of many fantasies, incorporating diverse influences—not only Romanesque, but Venetian and Moorish as well. One small detail that is easily overlooked is the name "Quincy Street" embedded in stone on the southeast corner of the building. But the real treat here—and this is why it is so important to visit the Rookery when the building is open—is the incredible inner court, a tour de force of design wrought in iron, copper, marble, glass, and terra-cotta, among other materials.

The Rookery is essentially a square built around an open interior court that rises the full height of the building's 11 stories. The ground and mezzanine levels, however, are covered by a lovely domed skylight (and now a second skylight has been added at roof level, for safety reasons, to enclose the entire light shaft). This two-tiered interior court is built around a gracefully curved cast-iron stairwell just beyond the small lobby, and a grand central staircase on the opposite wall, which are joined by a balcony at mezzanine level and encircled by a railing of delicate grillwork. Root's Victorian-style ornamentation throughout the light court was replaced in 1905 by Frank Lloyd Wright, who gave the space a more geometric look, replacing much of the original iron work, installing large rectangular planters, and replacing Root's terra-cotta cladding with a compound of gilded marble. During a recent renovation in which the Rookery's much altered exterior and interior were restored to their fin-de-siècle elegance, Wright's marble sheathing was stripped from one side of a column in the light court, revealing Root's original terra-cotta; the effect is to make Wright's marble covering look like sheetrock over richly textured horsehair plaster.

At Jackson Street, one block south, La Salle Street appears to

JOHN WELLBORN ROOT

Born in Georgia in 1850, Root was sent by his family to England to sit out the Civil War years in safety. Following a year at Oxford, Root returned to New York in 1866 and completed his studies at New York University, where he obtained a bachelor's degree in civil engineering in 1869.

Within two years, an unprecedented architectural boom was sweeping through Chicago with almost as much force as the disastrous fire that had leveled the city. Like so many ambitious young builders of the day who were eager to accomplish great works, Root rushed to Chicago to participate in this massive task of urban reconstruction.

By 1873, John W. Root had formed a partnership with another young draftsman, Daniel H. Burnham, that was to evolve into one of the most celebrated architectural firms in American history. In their collaboration, Burnham was considered the visionary businessman and Root the genius of design. The two lasting monuments in Chicago to Root's unique artistry are the Rookery and the Monadnock Building.

On New Year's Eve in 1891, Root and his wife hosted a party at their Gold Coast town house. Legend has it that the affable and well-bred Root insisted on escorting each of his guests to their waiting coaches at the end of the evening, despite the exceptionally bitter cold. Fifteen days later, John Wellborn Root was dead of pneumonia at age 41.

dead end (it actually jogs around to the east) before the imposing structure of the:

15. Chicago Board of Trade. Here at One Financial Place is the temple (or, more appropriately, the throne, as the building's general configuration suggests) of Chicago high finance, the house that corn and wheat built as westward migration transformed the great trans-Mississippi prairie into the nation's granary. On a more prosaic level, the Board of Trade shelters today that raucous free-for-all known as the commodity exchange, a kind of roller derby in pinstripes. The building also houses what is probably the best restaurant within Chicago's city limits, Everest, nestled high above the muck and mire of the trading pits in its top floor aerie, and offering, along with chef/proprietor Jean Joho's unique Alsatian cuisine, a most spectacular view of the Chicago skyline by night.

Opened in 1930, the 45-floor Board of Trade enjoyed the distinction of being the Loop's tallest building for 25 years, until it was eclipsed by the Prudential Building at 130 East Randolph Street. The setbacks of the Board of Trade's upper stories are typical of the art deco styling of the era, which is now strangely complemented by the 24-story post-modern addition flanking the building along its rear or southern wall, the work of Helmut Jahn. Symmetry is maintained between the older structure and the addition through the repetition of a pyramid-shaped roof, the principal feature common to both. In its day, the Board of Trade was considered so tall that the sleek steel sculpture adorning the building's peak was left faceless; it was reasoned that no one would ever get high enough in a neighboring building to see the face anyway.

Now head three blocks east along Jackson Street to the southwest corner of Dearborn and Jackson. There at 53 West Jackson Boulevard is the:

16. **Monadnock Building.** The two buildings formed from this mass of stonework occupy this entire narrow block all the way to Van Buren Street. Only two years separate the construction of these architectural gemini, but they are light years apart in design and engineering.

Monadnock I, on the northern end, was built by Burnham & Root between 1889 and 1891. Note the deeply recessed windows along the building at street level; they are encased in walls of masonry six to eight feet thick. The building's facade curls gently down from the roof line in what architects describe as a "papyrus" design, an accommodation in the proportion of a structure of this elevation that required extra thickness at the base to support it.

Monadnock II, on the southern wing, was built by Holabird & Roche in 1893. Continuity of design is maintained to some degree in this steel-framed building, but somehow the effect is less satisfying than the original.

Across the street, one block south at 343 South Dearborn Street, at the corner of Van Buren Street, is the:

17. **Fisher Building.** Daniel Burnham built this little gem in 1896 for a developer named Lucius Fisher. The yellow terra-cotta sheathing gives an attractive patina to the building's facade, as do the stern Gothic adornments. But Fisher ensured his own brand of immortality by having his architect include aquatic figures on the facade as well—delightful little fishes, snakes, shells, and crabs. Details worth seeing on the second floor are the original floor mosaics and the walls of Carrara marble. A bay was added to the building's north side in 1907, and seems to have

buttressed the older section, which leans perceptibly in that direction owing to its less than firm foundation.

Our stroll continues down Dearborn Street, taking in a few more priceless samples of old Chicago architecture as this tour nears its final stop. Across from the Fisher Building at 407 South Dearborn Street is the:

18. Old Colony Building. Plymouth Street runs parallel to Dearborn here, one block to the east. In its name, this street and the names of several vintage buildings throughout this old downtown section, we hear echoes of nostalgia for the New England origins of many pioneer Chicago families. The firm of Holabird & Roche completed the Old Colony in 1894. Among the building's standout features are the corner bays flanking the central tower, a variation on the tripartite design typical of many buildings of this era. The building's broad front gives a deceptive image of its bulk; when you turn the corner, you see it is only one bay wide. To achieve stability in the 17-story building, the architects included portal arches, a first in American construction.

At 431 South Dearborn Street, at the southwest corner of the Congress Expressway, is the:

19. Manhattan Building. Built in 1891 by William Le Baron Jenny, this broad structure was seen as an architectural wonder by many who visited Chicago during the Columbian Exposition two years later. To some, the eclectic use of materials and varied design of the facade give the Manhattan Building an appearance of complete chaos; others perceive a dynamic rhythm in the architect's choices. Whatever your aesthetic reaction, the Manhattan Building occupies a revered place in the annals of U.S. architecture, being the first 16-story building in America, and for a time the tallest building in the world. In 1982, the Manhattan Building was renovated to create 105 residential units.

Crossing the Congress Expressway, you now enter what is known as the South Loop, also called Burnham Park. Right on the southwest corner of this intersection at 500 South Dearborn Street is a wonderful small hotel, the Hyatt on Printer's Row, modern in appointments but European in scale and service. The Prairie restaurant is found in the same building, and is noted for the elegance of its heartland-inspired menu.

This final stretch of Dearborn Street is a veritable museum of old Chicago architecture, featuring many fine early industrial buildings. Collectively this area is referred to as Printers Row, and was once the center of Chicago's printing industry. In recent years, the neighborhood has become somewhat gentrified, and along the route as you proceed south, you will pass many interesting shops and eateries. When you arrive at Polk Street, Dearborn Street and our tour come to an end at the:

20. **Dearborn Station Galleria,** which can also serve as a final refueling stop. This is Chicago's oldest surviving railroad station, a U-shaped Romanesque structure with a central clock tower. Today the station houses a variety of retail galleries and food counters with café-style seating.

WALKING TOUR 2

South Michigan Avenue/Grant Park

Start: Chicago Cultural Center, 78 East Washington Street, at the corner of South Michigan Avenue.

Public Transportation: Take the Ravenswood or Lake/Dan Ryan lines to the Madison/Wabash stop. Buses passing along South Michigan Avenue or nearby thoroughfares include the numbers 3, 4, 60, 145, 147, or 151.

Finish: The Art Institute of Chicago, South Michigan Avenue at Adams Street.

Time: 2 to 4 hours.

Best Times: A warm, open-ended summer day or a weekend practically any time of year, weather permitting. If your walk will include actual visits to any of the museums and attractions listed in this itinerary, coordinate your plans in accordance with opening and closing times.

Worst Times: Only nighttime is unsuitable for this itinerary. No sensible person enters an urban park after dark (unless accompanied by a large multitude going to some event); the trolls might get you.

This walk follows Michigan Avenue south to Balbo Avenue, and is as close as you can get in Chicago to a stroll along a grand boulevard, with pauses for you to take in various sites of cultural, historical, and architectural interest. If you choose, you can then walk (or cab) about a mile south to visit the Field Museum, aquarium, and planetarium, returning virtually to our point of departure through Grant Park, the long patch of green space bordering Lake Michigan on one side and the Loop on the other. In its entirety, this walk not only provides a unique perspective on downtown Chicago, but takes visitors past the single largest concentration of cultural institutions in the city. You may decide to briefly "preview" some of these attractions now, or return later as interest and scheduling permits.

Begin at the:

1. **Chicago Cultural Center,** promoted as the "People's Palace." There are many reasons for entering what was formerly the main branch of the Chicago Public Library. The building itself dates from 1897, and its exterior can be appreciated as a monumental object of Renaissance proportions. Should you wish to venture inside, here's what you'll find:

   Enter from Washington Street and take in the workmanship of the lobby, whose splendor cannot be adequately described in a few brief superlatives; suffice it to say, the space is breathtaking. Most of the first floor of the Cultural Center on this side of the building houses the Museum of Broadcast Communications, which includes the Radio Hall of Fame and the Kraft TeleCenter. Access to the museum is free of charge.

   The grand central staircase in the lobby leads to the Preston Bradley Hall on the third floor, another exquisite space used frequently for free public concerts and other performances. A modern passageway enclosed in glass leads to the north half of the building. Straight ahead is the Theatre, used primarily for films and live performances and as a meeting hall. Adjacent to the Theatre is the G.A.R. (Grand Army of the Republic) Rotunda, a glorious and highly ornate leaded dome, formerly a skylight but now artificially backlit to allow for full appreciation of the dome's beauty and craftsmanship.

   The ground floor on the Randolph Drive side of the Cultural Center provides space for a large Gallery/Café where art from Chicago's neighborhoods is featured on a regular and rotating basis. To one side of the exhibit area is a dance studio used for rehearsals and free public performances.

REFUELING STOP The **Chicago Cultural Center Gallery/Café** is the perfect spot to hang out over a cup of gourmet coffee and a light snack while you get your bearings before plunging into this walking tour. The atmosphere is "café"

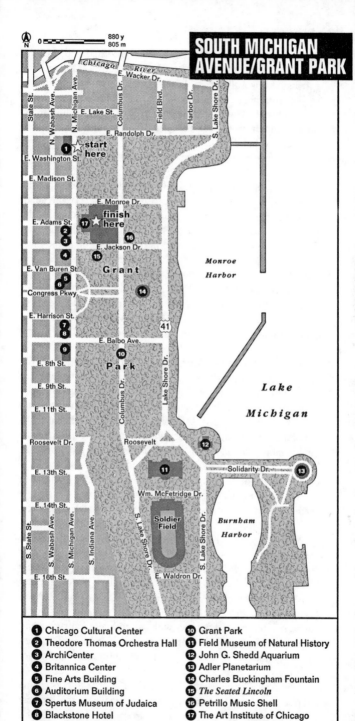

SOUTH MICHIGAN AVENUE/GRANT PARK

0 880 y / 805 m

N

Chicago River
E. Wacker Dr.
E. Lake St.
E. Randolph Dr.
E. Washington St.
start here
E. Madison St.
E. Monroe Dr.
finish here
E. Adams St.
E. Jackson Dr.
E. Van Buren St.
Congress Pkwy.
E. Harrison St.
E. Balbo Ave.
E. 8th St.
E. 9th St.
E. 11th St.
Roosevelt Dr.
E. 13th St.
E. 14th St.
E. 16th St.

State St.
N. Wabash Ave.
N. Michigan Ave.
Columbus Dr.
Field Blvd.
Harbor Dr.
S. Lake Shore Dr.

S. State St.
S. Wabash Ave.
S. Michigan Ave.
S. Indiana Ave.
Columbus Dr.
Lake Shore Dr.
S. Lake Shore Dr.

Grant Park

Monroe Harbor

Lake Michigan

41

Roosevelt

Wm. McFetridge Dr.

Soldier Field

E. Waldron Dr.

Solidarity Dr.

Burnham Harbor

- ❶ Chicago Cultural Center
- ❷ Theodore Thomas Orchestra Hall
- ❸ ArchiCenter
- ❹ Britannica Center
- ❺ Fine Arts Building
- ❻ Auditorium Building
- ❼ Spertus Museum of Judaica
- ❽ Blackstone Hotel
- ❾ Chicago Hilton & Towers
- ❿ Grant Park
- ⓫ Field Museum of Natural History
- ⓬ John G. Shedd Aquarium
- ⓭ Adler Planetarium
- ⓮ Charles Buckingham Fountain
- ⓯ *The Seated Lincoln*
- ⓰ Petrillo Music Shell
- ⓱ The Art Institute of Chicago

6559

in the best sense of the word—totally informal and pressure free. Many small tables with chairs are spread over a large area surrounded by walls of art. Beverages and a few food items are served from a cart here. The Chicago Cultural Center's hours are Monday to Thursday from 9am to 7pm, Friday from 9am to 6pm, Saturday from 9am to 5pm, and Sunday from noon to 5pm; closed holidays.

Walk south three blocks on Michigan Avenue and cross Adams Street. Along the way, you will pass several small buildings that might spark your curiosity. For example, the terra-cotta facade of the **Gage Building,** 18 South Michigan Avenue, was designed by Louis Sullivan at the behest of the Gage Brothers, who hoped that this burst of external beautification would "benefit" their millinery business. The gabled roof above the **Monroe Building,** 104 South Michigan Avenue, provides an eyecatching feature along the skyline. Take a peek inside here to see the vaulted lobby. At 220 South Michigan Avenue, you will be standing in front of the home of the Chicago Symphony, the:

2. **Theodore Thomas Orchestra Hall.** Believing that the Chicago Symphony needed a home of its own, rather than continuing to share space at the Auditorium Building down the block, Daniel Burnham designed this building, which opened its doors in 1905. The facade is Georgian, and inside, in addition to the orchestra hall, is a ballroom on the second floor, along with innumerable offices. With its official name, Orchestra Hall honors onetime violin prodigy Theodore Thomas, who is credited with founding symphony orchestras in many American cities—including Chicago's in 1898, where he was the first to premier the work of such contemporaries as Tchaikovsky, Brahms, and Johann Strauss.

Next door to Orchestra Hall at 224 South Michigan Avenue is the:

3. **ArchiCenter.** Here's a shop worth browsing given the largely historical and architectural nature of this walk. The ArchiCenter is the public face of the highly respected Chicago Architecture Foundation: a bookstore featuring titles on all your favorite Chicago builders; a gift shop with an architectural twist; and point of departure for many Foundation-sponsored guided tours conducted by a corps of highly informative volunteer docents.

The ArchiCenter is itself housed in a structure of some interest: the Santa Fe Center, known originally as the Railway Exchange Building, another work from the firm of D. H.

Burnham & Co. Like the Rookery, a principal design feature here is a two-story skylit atrium where the walls are clad with decorative tiles molded from terra-cotta.

Across Jackson Street at 310 South Michigan Avenue is the:

4. Britannica Center. The former Straus Building, sheathed in Indiana limestone, dates from 1924 and is now home to the Encyclopaedia Britannica Company. The setback windows conform to conditions required by a 1923 zoning ordinance that allowed buildings to rise above 260 feet for the first time in the city of Chicago. At night, the great glass beehive on the rooftop, symbol of the original banking firm, casts a blue light; the hive is surrounded by four bison representing thrift, industry, strength, and city.

Continue south for one and a half blocks, crossing Van Buren Street and stopping before 410 South Michigan Avenue, the:

5. Fine Arts Building. Perhaps no other building in Chicago has a more interesting and varied background. Originally called the Studebaker Building and serving as a showroom covering five floors for displaying that company's well-crafted carriages, it was constructed in 1885 by Solon S. Berman, the same man who laid out George Pullman's company town on the extreme southern edge of Chicago. In 1898, when the Studebaker Company vacated the building, it was converted into an arts center, with two theaters on the ground floor, plus work spaces for a whole spectrum of artists and writers, including skylit studios in a new three-story addition. Among the Fine Arts Building's illustrious tenants over the years were Frank Lloyd Wright, the sculptor Lorado Taft, and, according to some sources, L. Frank Baum, author of *The Wizard of Oz*.

Today, the building still houses many creative tenants, while the two theaters have been converted to four art movie houses. A few minutes spent walking around inside the building will reward you with some delightful visual treats, like the marble-and wood-trimmed lobby, and a series of wall murals on the 10th floor.

Directly next door to the Fine Arts Building is our next point of curiosity, 430 South Michigan Avenue, or the:

6. Auditorium Building. The team of Dankmar Adler and Louis Henri Sullivan were responsible for this landmark of fin de siècle Chicago architecture. In a sense, theirs was a perfect partnership: Adler was a man of nuts-and-bolts business acumen, whereas Sullivan was a visionary of design. The staying power of their achievement and the Auditorium Building's elevated reputation rests on several factors. When it opened in 1889, the Auditorium was one of Chicago's first multi-use buildings; originally, it contained a fine hotel, a theater, and, in a 17-story tower perched above the southwest corner of the roof, some of the most high-priced office space in the city.

In its sheer mass—the building spreads the entire distance between Michigan Avenue and Wabash—and its patently Richardsonesque monumental scale rising above a rusticated granite base, the Auditorium Building's general appearance is palpable testimony to the influence H. R. Richardson had over many architectural disciples, including John Wellborn Root and Louis Sullivan. In this case, however, Sullivan's refined exterior work, the arched windows and other details of form that grace the Auditorium's facade, owe their greatest debt to the solid structural innovations introduced by his partner, Dankmar Adler, who perfected his own craft while serving the Union Army as an engineer during the Civil War.

Some of Adler's most original contributions involved engineering features within the theater itself, whose inauguration transformed this rough-cut city, still struggling to resurrect itself from the fire that had nearly brought on its demise some two decades before, into a viable cultural center with international credentials. Adler had encased the 4,300-seat theater in a shell of firebrick, and configured the interior space in such a way that the sightlines and acoustics are still the envy of many modern entertainment halls. A wide stage with elaborate hydraulic equipment enhanced the epic quality of many performances, which had to be spectacular indeed to rival the beauty of Sullivan's decor, a dazzling spectacle in its own right. The Auditorium Theater is still an important cultural venue in Chicago, and tours of its interior are conducted regularly. For information on scheduling, call 922-4046.

Since 1949, the Auditorium Building has been occupied by Roosevelt University, so you're guaranteed access to some of the grand features of the former hotel during hours when classes are in session. The university library, for example, today occupies the barrel-vaulted salon on the 10th floor that was formerly the hotel's dining room, and is yet another showcase of the handiwork of Sullivan's gifted artisans.

Our tour continues south for another two blocks before entering Grant Park, so you can now cross Congress Parkway. Looking back, you may be able to notice where the southern end of the original Auditorium Building, once the site of the hotel's long and elegant barroom, was demolished to make room for the expanded roadway. Another block down, across Harrison Street in one wing of Columbia College at 600 South Michigan Avenue, is the Museum of Contemporary Photography, open to the public free of charge. Several doors down at 618 South Michigan Avenue is the:

THE STUDEBAKER BROTHERS

How many of our younger citizens have even heard of an automobile company called Studebaker, which once manufactured those funny, sausage-shaped cars in the late 1940s and early '50s? Yet there was a time—certainly when the Fine Arts Building was constructed in 1885—when the name "Studebaker" symbolized first-rate quality in the manufacture of fine horse-driven carriages.

The founder of the company, Clement Studebaker, grew up in rural Pennsylvania during the mid-1800s, a descendant in a line of Old World wagon makers who had migrated to William Penn's colony a century before. By 1852, Clement Studebaker was in South Bend, Indiana, where he established a blacksmith and wagon shop. As his forefathers had done before him among the Pennsylvania Dutch farmers, Clement and his brother John now began to supply sturdy wagons for the surrounding agricultural communities of the Midwest. A lucrative Civil War contract provided sufficient capital to launch the Studebakers, a partnership now including all five male siblings, into the national market. Their first branch office was opened in 1870 in St. Joseph, Missouri, where the firm aided in the outfitting of pioneers who were settling the West. During its wagon-making days, the Studebaker Company produced over 750,000 horse-drawn vehicles.

The Studebakers began manufacturing automobiles in the late 1890s, and for several decades they prospered. While somewhat eccentric in design, their cars had a reputation for performance and craftsmanship. In 1954, however, the company was forced to merge with Packard, and in 1963 to cease production entirely. One arcane note in the history of the Studebaker car involves the names of its models in 1934: the Commander, the President, and . . . the Dictator.

7. **Spertus Museum of Judaica.** Housed in the same building as the Spertus College of Judaica and the Asher Library, the museum's collection of some 3,000 works offers the public a sweeping view of Jewish culture as it has evolved over more than three millennia. Items on display include ceremonial objects, textiles and costumes, jewelry, coins, paintings, sculpture, and graphics from around the world. Many Chicago area schools make use of workshops, films, and other resources at the Spertus Museum's Zell Memorial to comply with a 1990 state law

mandating Holocaust education in all Illinois public schools Other programs at the museum include weekend film and lecture series. Hours are Sunday to Thursday from 10am to 5pm, Friday from 10am to 3pm, closed Saturday; there is an admission fee.

The next cross street continuing south is Balbo, where we will enter Grant Park. But first, take in the graceful old structure on the corner at 636 South Michigan Avenue, the:

8. Blackstone Hotel. There are several reasons for calling this old hotel to your attention. The Blackstone's palatial exterior is a treat for the eyes, and the opulence of its lobby, which you may enter for a brief digression, recalls a bygone era when hotel elegance was taken for granted.

The Blackstone has also made its appearance in the world of literature and film. James T. Farrell used the hotel as a setting for a New Year's Eve party in his *Studs Lonigan,* a trilogy about the lives of the Chicago Irish during the early years of the century. And more recently, the savage banquet scene in the movie *The Untouchables* was shot here, evoking the style of a similar hotel a few miles south, the Metropole, where Al Capone once resided and where such an event might have actually taken place. Finally, some of the best jazz in the city, especially of the bebop variety, may still be heard at Joe Segal's Jazz Showcase, an institution ensconced within the Blackstone for many years.

Now cross Balbo and check out the old Conrad Hilton, the first name in hotel swank throughout much of this century at 720 South Michigan Avenue, and known today as the:

9. Chicago Hilton & Towers. The Hilton is truly a relic from the final days of the age of grandeur, a time when "putting on the Ritz" was considered the best revenge in a world of crumbling economic fortunes. Built as the Stevens Hotel in 1927 with 3,000 rooms, it was then the largest hotel in the world. Among its extravagant amenities, the Stevens offered its guests a 1,200-seat theater equipped for movie "talkies," a private in-house hospital, an indoor ice rink, and a rooftop that included two gardens and the 18-hole High Ho Golf Course.

Today, these services have gone the way of all such excesses of the super-rich. But the modern Hilton, renovated at a cost of $185 million in 1985, is nothing to sneeze at. It's definitely worth a few moments to wander into the lobby, and walk around a public space of rare elegance and dimension.

Crossing South Michigan Avenue at the corner of Balbo, our walking tour will now double back on itself via:

10. Grant Park. In July 1968, Norman Mailer, in town to cover the Democratic Presidential Convention, looked out from the window of his room in the Chicago Hilton, and reflected on the presence of so many thousands of anti–Vietnam War protestors who were at that moment encamped in Grant Park, otherwise known as "Chicago's formal front garden." And that brief episode, in a nutshell, sums up Grant Park's essential urban function: It is not so much a green space that imitates the idyllic environment of a woods or forest, but a checkerboard of great lawns, criss-crossed by broad roadways and train tracks, that serves as a giant outdoor arena for mass public events. Over a 10-week period in the summertime, for example, popular outdoor concerts are staged in the park every Wednesday, Friday, Saturday, and Sunday evening. These and other seasonal public festivals justify so many empty acres, which otherwise are not terribly parklike.

For our purposes, however, the park—especially on a quiet, non-festival day—provides a contrast to the sidewalk strolling that has occupied the first half of this tour, and, from its middle ground, you'll get a rather eerie perspective on the city, as if you were viewing the skyline of the Loop from a distant shore.

Enter the park along East Balbo Drive, and walk the long block to the first wide thoroughfare, South Columbus Drive. Here you have the option of walking the better part of a mile (the foot-weary should consider a taxi) to the southern extreme of the park to see or visit three of Chicago's most popular cultural institutions, or of returning north through the park to our tour's point of origin (pick up this tour at stop 14 if you choose to skip the southern end of Grant Park).

Should you choose to walk south, the first building among the triad of cultural attractions is the:

11. Field Museum of Natural History. Combining a somewhat old-fashioned view of nature as a giant curio shop with a contemporary emphasis on interactive showmanship, the Field is undoubtedly one of Chicago's most fascinating museums. Even on a walking tour one could justify paying the price of admission and making a cursory inspection of the exhibits, enjoying whatever the eye can absorb during a brief visit. If, however, you choose to remain outside, at least pause before the monumental temple that houses this collection of human and natural artifacts to appreciate the harmony of its classical design. Daniel Burnham began the work around 1909, and derived his inspiration, as the telling line of Ionic columns confirms, from the Erechtheum (ca. 400 B.C.), one of the great shrines adorning the Acropolis in Athens. The museum is open daily from 9am to 5pm; closed Thanksgiving, Christmas, and New Year's Day.

Directly east of the Field Museum, a short walk away, is an enterprise that is rapidly becoming the most popular tourist attraction in all Chicago, the:

12. **John G. Shedd Aquarium.** There's a fantasy quality to the building that houses the aquarium, with its dozens of decorative aquatic figures, but the meteoric rise in the attraction's popularity is due to the 1991 addition of the Oceanarium, a marine mammal pavilion that re-creates a Pacific Northwest coastal environment, with a curtain wall at one end that incorporates Lake Michigan into its watery motif. Open daily from 9am to 6pm; admission is charged.

Connected to the Shedd Aquarium in spirit, if not theme, on the east end of ornamental Solidarity Drive, a manmade causeway extending to a landfill island known as Northerly Island, is the:

13. **Adler Planetarium.** The zodiacal, 12-sided dome sits on a promontory facing the runway of its co-tenant on this artificial landmass, Miegs Field, an in-town airfield for small planes. Within the planetarium, through a variety of programs, the night sky is brought into sharper focus for the human eye. The Sky Show is offered daily; call 322-0300 for current times.

Now return to the vicinity of East Balbo Drive, along any one of three possible routes, Columbus Drive, through the park itself, or along Lake Shore Drive, the route running closest to Lake Michigan. Just north of Balbo Drive, you will see the approach to the:

14. **Charles Buckingham Fountain.** This baroque fountain constructed in pink marble is the centerpiece of Grant Park, modeled after (but twice as large as) the Latona Fountain on the grounds of Versailles. Throughout the late spring and summer, the fountain spurts columns of water up to 100 feet in the air, illuminated after dark by a whirl of colored lights.

Return now to Columbus Drive and walk roughly half the distance between Congress Parkway and Jackson, the next street to the north. On your left, between Columbus Drive and the railroad tracks of the Illinois Central is:

15. **The Seated Lincoln.** In what was originally planned to be a Court of the Presidents, this solitary likeness of Abraham Lincoln sits alone, the work in 1908 of the talented, enigmatic American sculptor, Augustus Saint Gaudens.

Continue north and cross East Jackson Drive. Nestled in the northeast corner of this intersection is the:

16. **Petrillo Music Shell.** This single location probably attracts more Chicago residents and visitors to Grant Park on a given evening in late spring or summer than any other attraction in the park. The free outdoor Blues (June) and Jazz Festivals (around Labor Day) alone account for vast multitudes of music lovers who crowd into the seats provided or take their leisure elsewhere on the surrounding grounds.

REFUELING STOP   While not confined to the area around the bandstand, another yearly outdoor event at the park, **Taste of Chicago,** would make an excellent refueling stop—but only if you happen to be here during an eight-day period spanning the last week of June and the first week of July. During the Taste of Chicago extravaganza, scores of Chicago restaurants cart their fare to foodstands set up throughout the park.

Walk one block north to Monroe Drive, where, among the complex of buildings on your left, we approach our final stop:

17. The Art Institute of Chicago. Before walking back to Michigan Avenue along Monroe Street, however, the first building you come to on Columbus Drive is the highly respected **Goodman Theater,** built in 1926 by the Chicago architect Howard Van Doren Shaw. Also along Columbus Drive, installed in a 1977 addition to the museum, is the actual Trading Room of the Old Chicago Stock Exchange, a work of Adler and Sullivan, salvaged at the time of the building's demolition. One wag refers to this exhibit as "the Wailing Wall of Chicago's preservationists."

The entrance to the museum itself is on South Michigan Avenue and Adams Street, at the top of the imposing steps flanked by two formidable bronze lions. As a building, the Art Institute of Chicago is a major Chicago landmark. The building was constructed at the time of the World's Columbian Exposition as a venue for conferences among the fair's participants; today, it contains one of the world's great collections of antiquities, paintings, and sculpture.

Wicker Park

Start: Intersection of North Milwaukee and West North avenues with North Damen Avenue.

Public Transportation: Take the A or B train to the Damen Avenue stop on the O'Hare/Congress/Douglas route.

Finish: The Busy Bee Restaurant, 1546 North Damen Avenue, essentially at the point of departure.

Time: 2 to 3 hours.

Best Times: Any time during the day.

Worst Times: At night.

Wicker Park, a mere 15-minute ride from downtown on the El out North Milwaukee Avenue, began as an immigrant neighborhood around 1870. Here middle-class artisans, mostly Germans and Scandinavians, were joined by a few dozen wealthy families among their countrymen, whose fortunes could justify luxurious homes and lifestyles, but whose foreign roots made them unwelcome or uncomfortable among their Anglo-American counterparts who were at that time taking up residence along the Gold Coast.

During the neighborhood's heyday, a 20-year span between 1870 and 1890, the foreign born constituted 44% of Chicago's population; among residents of Wicker Park, the foreign-born element during those same years climbed from 63% to an astonishing 96%.

The homes built by these successful entrepreneurs near Wicker

Park, many of which have been preserved, were renowned for their grace and eclectic styling. The neighborhood has undergone many transformations over the years, from lace-curtain respectability to rooming-house shabbiness to immigrant way station of the working poor. Today Wicker Park is home to a multiracial community, and a slow process of gentrification has gradually restored some of its landmark houses to their former stateliness. The entire neighborhood, including the commercial buildings along Milwaukee Avenue, appears much the way it did at the turn of the century.

The names of many notable families and personalities are historically associated with Wicker Park. Two of the great family fortunes of Chicago had their origins here, the Pritzkers and the Crowns. (Aire Crown, a Lithuanian Jew, once sold suspenders along Milwaukee Avenue.) Carl Laemmle, founder of Universal Studios, and Mike Todd, the Hollywood director, both lived here, as did authors Nelson Algren, Saul Bellow, and Studs Terkel. Wicker Park has been designated a historic landmark area and has been placed on the National Register of Historic Places.

To begin our tour, walk south one block along Damen Avenue to the edge of:

1. **Wicker Park,** the smallest park in Chicago. The land was donated to the city by two brothers who were beginning to develop their extensive real estate holdings in the area around 1870. By setting aside this four-acre plot as a greenspace or common, Charles Wicker, an alderman from the 3rd Ward who made his money building railroads, and his brother Joel, a lawyer and bank director, hoped to make their development more attractive to potential builders and investors. Apparently their strategy was successful. Very little remains of the park's 19th-century landscaping, which once included a large manmade pond spanned by a rustic bridge.

    Cross the park to the corner of Damen Avenue and Schiller Street. We will follow Schiller the length of the park, walking east. The first stop is:

2. **1959–1961 West Schiller Street.** Built in 1886 for a ship's captain and a medical doctor, this double home reflects the fashionable Second Empire style. The building became a rooming house in the 1920s, but has been restored in recent years. Note the lively Victorian colors of the cornices, the tower, and the trim. Other distinctive features are the large mansard roof and the decorative sawtooth pattern in the brickwork.

    Next we move to:

3. **1951 West Schiller Street.** When Dr. Nels T. Quales, a native of Norway, had this house built in 1873, he opted for

Italianate styling with a Romanesque Revival facade, most notable in the use of arches and truncated columns. Originally, the house was set back much farther from the street. The facade was altered around 1890 by the addition of Moorish windows on the first and second stories. Dr. Quales was a humanitarian who founded Chicago's Lutheran Deaconess Hospital; for this and his many other good works, he was awarded the Order of St. Olaf by the King of Norway in 1910.

At 1941 West Schiller Street, pause before the:

4. Harris Cohn House, also known as the Wicker Park Castle. Mr. Cohn was a clothing manufacturer who commissioned this piece of domestic fantasy in 1888. Behind an iron fence that was salvaged from the playground of one of Chicago's oldest public schools sits a white limestone structure that is essentially Queen Anne in design, and was a bit more pricey to construct in its day than most of the neighboring buildings. The rusticated facade features columns of granite, heavily polished to look like marble, and a turret that rests on a shell-shaped base. The stonework on the second-floor balcony follows a checkerboard pattern, and the handrails are scrolled with a motif of oak leaves. That cornice you see is not stone, but fabricated with sheet metal, a cost and fire safety compromise employed on many homes in the area.

On the corner is the former:

5. Serbian Eastern Orthodox Church. This pretty cream-colored building occupying 1905 West Schiller Street is still in service to religion. Today the church, which occupies the triangular point where Schiller intersects with Evergreen Avenue, belongs to a Puerto Rican congregation of the Christian Pentecostal Church.

At this corner, double back behind the church on Evergreen, and stop in front of:

6. 1958 West Evergreen Avenue. The house is interesting for much of its exterior decor, including the stonework—like the griffin in the keystone on the first floor, the urn with its sunflower on the second floor, and also the bas-relief of little cupids. But more interesting is the fact that novelist Nelson Algren (1909–1981) once lived here in a third-floor apartment from 1959 to 1975. Algren today is best remembered for his two dark novels of the urban semi-underworld, *A Walk on the Wild Side* and *The Man with the Golden Arm* (the latter of which was set near here around Division and Milwaukee), and for his tough but lyrical prose poem, *Chicago, City on the Make*.

The next stop is optional, for it takes us off the beaten path of this tour by a block or two. Still, the digression is justified, not because of the home you will look at, but because of who once lived there. At the corner of Evergreen and Damen avenues,

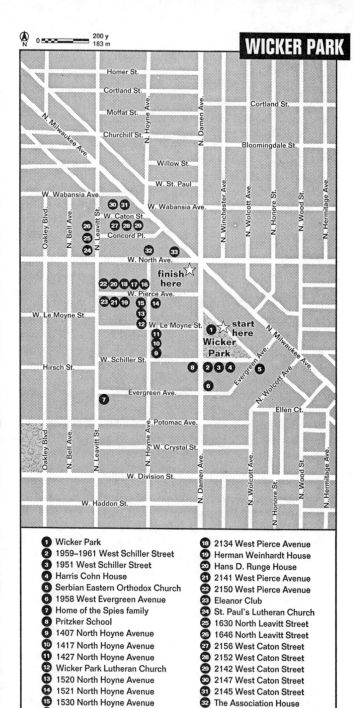

WICKER PARK

0 ——— 200 y
N 0 ——— 183 m

1. Wicker Park
2. 1959–1961 West Schiller Street
3. 1951 West Schiller Street
4. Harris Cohn House
5. Serbian Eastern Orthodox Church
6. 1958 West Evergreen Avenue
7. Home of the Spies family
8. Pritzker School
9. 1407 North Hoyne Avenue
10. 1417 North Hoyne Avenue
11. 1427 North Hoyne Avenue
12. Wicker Park Lutheran Church
13. 1520 North Hoyne Avenue
14. 1521 North Hoyne Avenue
15. 1530 North Hoyne Avenue
16. 1558 North Hoyne Avenue
17. 2118 West Pierce Avenue
18. 2134 West Pierce Avenue
19. Herman Weinhardt House
20. Hans D. Runge House
21. 2141 West Pierce Avenue
22. 2150 West Pierce Avenue
23. Eleanor Club
24. St. Paul's Lutheran Church
25. 1630 North Leavitt Street
26. 1646 North Leavitt Street
27. 2156 West Caton Street
28. 2152 West Caton Street
29. 2142 West Caton Street
30. 2147 West Caton Street
31. 2145 West Caton Street
32. The Association House
33. Luxor Baths

where you should take note of the storefront shop called Myopic Books and Coffee, turn left and head south one block to Potomac. Turn right and walk west for a block and a half, stopping at 2132 West Potomac, the:

7. **home of the Spies family.** At 10 o'clock on the morning of November 13, 1887, the coffin of August Spies was loaded onto a wagon beginning a funeral procession that some sources claim was witnessed by as many as one million onlookers as it proceeded down Milwaukee Avenue toward the train station in downtown Chicago. Spies, a German-born leader of the Chicago trade union movement and editor of the newspaper *Arbeiter-Zeitung,* was one of four men who had been hanged two days earlier in what is now regarded as one of the greatest miscarriages of justice in American history, the execution of the Haymarket Martyrs.

From here, the cortege would wind its way through the Wicker Park neighborhood, down Damen Avenue to Evergreen Avenue and over to Milwaukee Avenue, ultimately picking up the remains of four other Haymarket co-defendants, three of whom had suffered the same grim fate as Spies, while the other was alleged to have committed suicide on the day prior to the execution.

Return now to Damen Avenue and Schiller Street; across from the southern end of the park at 2009 West Schiller Street is the:

8. **Pritzker School.** The school is named for A. N. Pritzker, who grew up in the neighborhood, the son of a Russian immigrant, and graduated there when it was known as the Wicker Park School. When the Chicago School Board cut the school's funds for after-school programs, Pritzker set up a foundation to fund activities, and brought celebrities like Ernie Banks and the Harlem Globetrotters with him when he came to visit his alma mater. Within five years of having set up his foundation, the school's crime rate had dropped by 90%. In a break with Chicago School Board regulations, the community was allowed to honor Pritzker by renaming the school for him while he was still living.

Continue west along Schiller Street to North Hoyne Avenue, one of the first paved streets in the city of Chicago, where people came from miles around to roller skate on Sunday afternoons. All of Hoyne Avenue, from Evergreen Avenue to North Avenue, is known as Beer Baron Row. Most of the fine homes here were built by wealthy merchants during the 1880s and 1890s. Turn right, stopping at:

9. **1407 North Hoyne Avenue.** Built by German wine and beer merchant John H. Rapp in 1880, this was the largest single-

A CLOSER LOOK AT THE HAYMARKET AFFAIR

By the last quarter of the 19th century, the American labor movement was picking up steam. Concerted action by workers in many trades was beginning to pay off with better working conditions and higher wages. Chicago, with its huge blue-collar immigrant population, was a hotbed of labor activism. And on May 3, 1886, a rally before the McCormick Reaper Plant calling for an "eight-hour day" ended in violence. Two hundred police, under the command of a notoriously anti-labor police inspector, attacked the noisy but peaceful assembly of 6,000, leaving two workers dead and many injured.

A protest of this outrage was scheduled for the following evening at Haymarket Square near Randolph and Desplaines streets. Toward the end of the demonstration, when only a few hundred protestors remained, the police arrived and once again went on the attack. At this point, a bomb was hurled from the shadows, and a policeman fell. A small battle ensued with an exchange of gunfire between workers and the police. When the smoke cleared, seven policemen and four workers lay dead, and the wounded amounted to more than 60.

August Spies had spoken at the rally, but had left before the riot. Along with Spies, seven other labor leaders and activists, only two of whom had actually been present at Haymarket that night, were arrested and tried under vague conspiracy charges. Seven were condemned to die, two of whom had their sentences commuted to life imprisonment. The true identity of the bomb thrower never came to light during the trial, and it is only in recent years that a descendant of the assassin, one George Meng, has come forward to reveal his name. The lives of five men, two of whom were exceptional leaders of the Chicago labor movement, Spies and Albert Parsons, were thus extinguished by an act of judicial murder. Illinois Governor John Peter Altgeld arrived at the same conclusion, and pardoned the remaining Haymarket defendants in 1893, shortly after taking office. There is a monument to the Haymarket Martyrs in the old German Waldheim Cemetery, now called Forest Home, which is not far from the suburb of Oak Park.

family estate in Wicker Park. The coach house, behind the mansion, at 2044 West Schiller Street, is now a separate residence. This was not a happy home. Mrs. Rapp went insane, a son was convicted of embezzlement, and Rapp himself was murdered by his female bookkeeper. The house itself is of the Second Empire style, with a large, curbed mansard roof. The wrought iron fence is original, and still defines the boundaries of the original grounds. In 1920 the estate was sold and converted to four flats. In the neighborhood, this place is often referred to as the Goldblatt or Wieboldt Mansion, though no one from either of these great Chicago mercantile families—who were indeed residents of Wicker Park—ever lived here.

Our next point of interest is:

10. **1417 North Hoyne Avenue.** This appealingly overgrown property once belonged to Carl Wernecke, who built it in 1879. The rolling landscape was deliberate, created to simulate an asymmetrical meadow. The house is Italianate in style, and has unusually high windows on the first floor. Note the richly tooled woodwork on the side porch, especially the columns; this appendage was used, not as an entryway, but strictly for gazing upon the splendors of the garden in bloom.

Across the street at 1426 North Hoyne Street is a good example of a workingman's cottage, and a reminder that in these old immigrant neighborhoods, artisans and their patrons often lived side by side.

The next house down is:

11. **1427 North Hoyne Avenue.** The former home of a Norwegian furniture manufacturer, built in the late 1880s, this house typifies a phenomenon in the construction business of this era, when homes were designed piecemeal from a variety of pattern books. Many elements in eclectic homes of this type were simply ordered prefab. This house is primarily Romanesque, but incorporates other elements as well, such as Queen Anne. There is nothing prefab about the workmanship on the Scandinavian woodworker's porch, however. The bay of the porch is a combination of wood and pressed metal, a technique that came into fashion after the Great Fire of 1871.

On the next corner, at 1502 North Hoyne Avenue and LeMoyne is the:

12. **Wicker Park Lutheran Church.** Quaintly known as "the church with a heart in the heart of Chicago," it is also the city's oldest permanent Lutheran Church. The building was modeled from plans of Holy Trinity Church in Caen, France, dating from the 12th century. The stone for this Romanesque structure was recycled from a bawdy house on South Michigan Avenue, which had been torn down. To one of his scandalized parishioners, the

pastor remarked that the building material "has served the devil long enough; now let it serve the Lord."

Now walk on to:

13. **1520 North Hoyne Avenue.** A lumber merchant named Henry Grusendorf built this estate spanning two city lots in 1887. French Empire in design, the house—now containing two apartments—retains many of its original features, including four fireplaces. Inside, the ceilings rise to almost 14 feet, and are decorated with ornate plasterwork and moldings. Note the double-gabled "Queen" porch, the jeweled and stained-glass windows, and especially the anatomical forms supporting the banisters on the front stairs—cast-iron replicas of human hands. This is one of the few grand homes in Wicker Park that was never converted into a rooming house.

Directly across the street is:

14. **1521 North Hoyne Avenue.** The fatted calf of war profiteering, according to some, allowed Isaac Waixel to build this residence, ca. 1890, after he grossed a cool $20 million by selling beef to the federal government during the Civil War. Another faction among the historico-architects claims a more prosaic origin for this home at the hands of the German master chairmaker, later manufacturing executive, Adolph Borgmeier. By general agreement, however, the fetching workmanship, both inside and outside, was Borgmeier's handiwork. The building's design combines elements of Queen Anne and Romanesque styles, while the metal trim is rife with decorative symbols: rosettes, flowers and scrolls, dentils, and scrolled Ionic columns in relief on the dormer. Note also the likeness of a woman carved into the exterior, a typical embellishment on German-built houses. The market price of this house, incidentally, was around $700,000 in 1990.

Across the alley from the above address was the site of the original Schlitz Mansion, demolished in the 1920s to make room for the utilitarian yellow brick apartment building you see before you. The beer magnate once owned the entire block, running along Pierce Avenue to Damen Avenue, before moving his brewery to Milwaukee. Next we move across the street to:

15. **1530 North Hoyne Avenue.** Noted more for its former residents than as a site of architectural interest, this home was once occupied by William Leger, a newspaperman and Democratic Party activist, who coined the phrase "Beer Baron Row." Leger himself rose from the ad department of a German-language daily to become president of two local brewing companies. Later, German architect Hermann Gaul, who is known for having designed many churches in Chicago—including St. Michael's, St. Benedict's, St. Matthias, St. Raphael,

and many more—lived here from 1912 to 1939 with his wife and their 10 children.

This corner of Pierce and Hoyne was, in its day, one of the most fashionable addresses in the city. Cross Pierce Avenue and continue on the left side of the street, past the Urban Garden Plot, to:

16. **1558 North Hoyne Avenue.** The building permit for this Queen Anne–style home was issued in 1877, making it one of the oldest homes in this area. It was built for C. Hermann Plautz, founder of the Chicago Drug and Chemical Company in 1861, president of the Northwestern Brewing Company, and later city treasurer of Chicago. Ever conscious of the Chicago Fire, the builders created all the decorative trim on both towers, the cornices, and the conservatory of the south side from ornamental pressed metal. The seemingly misplaced cannon in the front yard is a relic of the years, 1927 to 1972, when the building housed the local American Legion, who used the former 800-square-foot living room as their meeting hall. The landscaping followed an 1870 Victorian garden book, and the garden contains a weeping juniper and a Norway dwarf spruce.

Now return to Pierce Avenue once more and walk west to:

17. **2118 West Pierce Avenue.** This French chateau–style home with neoclassical elements was built for Theodore Noel, a drug company executive, in 1903. The dormer is Gothic Revival, and the pineapple frieze, a symbol of hospitality. The slate sidewalk in front of the house is original.

Two doors down is:

18. **2134 West Pierce Avenue.** Also vaguely French chateau, this structure was constructed in 1903 for Theodore's brother Joseph Noel, a banker, by the same team who built no. 2118. Notable details on the facade here are the twisting bands, or guilloche pattern, that resolve the framing, and the bay-leaf garland molding hanging from the second story. For some time during the 1940s the house served as a residence for a local settlement house, which we will visit further on (see Stop 32, below). Today, it contains two apartments.

Across the street is 2137 West Pierce Avenue, the:

19. **Hermann Weinhardt House.** This well-preserved gem is certainly one of the highlights of the tour. Any further evidence that German culture does not entirely fall within the tradition of the West is not required once you have taken in the oriental fantasy manifested by the outline of this extraordinary structure, built in 1888. Weinhardt was a manufacturer and a West Park Commissioner, and one critic referred to his creation as a "Victorian gingerbread design"; but in truth, the house defies identity with any genre. The charm is in the whole, but among

the notable details are the elaborate balcony of carved wood facing east, and the unusual juxtaposition of green stone and red brick limestone, which creates a singular effect around the large front window. This lot is sizeable and was once flooded annually for ice skating. Yet the core of the house, when the porches are omitted, is quite narrow, like the neighboring workers' cottages. Its three stories, however, sit astride an English basement, where the kitchen is still in use for everyday dining.

Of interest both historically and architecturally is 2138 West Pierce Avenue, the:

20. Hans D. Runge House. Runge was treasurer of the Wolf Brothers Wood Milling Company, and his home, built in 1884, is considered one of the best surviving examples in the area of the Eastlake style of ornamentation of porch posts, balusters, railings, and so forth. The style takes its name from Charles Locke Eastlake, a 19th-century English interior designer. As to the overall design, various styles have been suggested: Swiss chalet, Viennese cottage, and carpenter's steamboat. Elaborate wood carving characterizes the house both inside and out; among the unique designs are the Masonic symbols flanking the dragon's head under the rounded arch. The house was subsequently owned by a well-heeled local banker and politician, John F. Smulski, who acquired it in 1902, about the time many Poles were moving into the neighborhood. Smulski committed suicide here after the stock market crash in 1929, and the house served for a time as the Polish consulate. On one memorable occasion, the great pianist—and onetime prime minister of Poland for a brief span after World War I—Ignacy Paderewski treated the neighborhood to a concert from the upper level of the elegant two-story front porch in the 1930s.

Across the street is:

21. 2141 West Pierce Avenue. The prelate of Chicago's Ukrainian Church once occupied this home from 1954 to 1971, as the presence of the Eastern Cross atop the roof still testifies. But the early Queen Anne structure was originally built for Theodore Daniel Juergens, whose Horatio Alger life saw him climb from the jobs of telegraph operator, sign painter, and decorator to the presidency of the American Varnish Company. Gargoyle fans will enjoy the grotesque figures leering down at them from above the original finial and at the corners of the house. Facing the garden on the east side is the first-floor conservatory, and on the third floor, there was a ballroom for formal entertainments.

An interesting relic of the pre-automotive world remains at curbside before:

22. 2150 West Pierce Avenue. The stepping stone near the driveway was used when visitors descended here at the curb from a horse and carriage. The inscription "J. C. Horn" enshrines the name of the original owner, a furniture manufacturer and president of the Horn Bros. Manufacturing Company. This house is just one of several faithful examples of the once-popular rusticated Romanesque look. Among the houses of this genre nearby are nos. 2146 and 2156, the latter home to another rag-to-riches success story, August Lempke, a peddler who became vice president of a coal company and state fish commissioner.

The large building across the street is now a nursing home. Until 1960, however, it was a branch of the:

23. Eleanor Club. These were respectable dormitories in Chicago for single working women. In the early years, residents received room plus breakfast and dinner for $6.50 a week. Living conditions were commodious, and included a variety of common spaces such as homelike parlors and living rooms, a roof garden, sleeping porch, sewing room, library, and laundry.

Turn right onto Leavitt Street and walk to North Avenue. The church on the west side of the street at 2215 West North Avenue is the former:

24. St. Paul's Lutheran Church. The original congregation was founded in 1873, and this building went up almost 20 years later. Services were in Norwegian until 1903. If you could get inside the church, which has been for sale since 1990, you'd see an interior of elaborate woodwork carved to create the illusion of being in an ark. The first pipe organ installed by the Austin Company in Chicago was built here in 1906.

Cross North Avenue and continue up Leavitt Street to Concord. The lots here are smaller because this area was developed later when land was already at a premium, and most of the newcomers were Scandinavians rather than Germans. One novelty not to be missed is:

25. 1630 North Leavitt Street. This clapboard farmhouse was moved to this site in 1914. To spruce up the structure, the porch, bays, and leaded glass were added at this present location.

Closer to Caton Street is:

26. 1646 North Leavitt Street. This home was built for Fred A. Miller in 1897 and, with its fine stonework, represents the beaux arts style of architecture. Over the entrance is an unusual oval window of bevelled glass, and the beaded molding surrounding the door is also worthy of note. The house has been restored in recent years, which was not a cheap proposition. The restoration of the cornice alone was said to cost $16,000.

Many of the houses on Caton Street were built in the early 1890s by the same architectural firm, Faber and Pagel, each according to a different fantasy and style. Walking toward Milwaukee Avenue, the numbers go in descending order. The first house of interest is:

27. 2156 West Caton Street. An import-export entrepreneur, Ole Thorpe, built this and the three houses adjacent to it around 1892. At the time, his project was known as the Thorpe subdivision. This house, no. 2156, is described as a German Burgher manse, though its fireplace is adorned with the crest of Norway. There's also a terrazzo floor in the basement-level ballroom. On the outside, the most obvious feature is the heavy domed turret rising from the flared and rusticated foundations. There are also many stained-glass windows, including one on the side topped with a half-moon lunette. And don't miss the sunburst design over the door on the second-story porch.

Continuing a few steps to the east, we come to:

28. 2152 West Caton Street. The original owner of this 1891 home was a livery contractor named Max Tauber. He had the largest stable operation in the city, and was also a crony of the mayor's. The house was described as Renaissance, while the melodrama enfolding within its walls during Tauber's tenure was decidedly Byzantine, with an American twist. When hearing the erroneous news that Max had died in a fire at work, his first wife succumbed to a heart attack. Max took a new wife in the 1920s, then lost his shirt in the stock market crash of 1929. Eschewing the option of declaring bankruptcy, he formed a partnership in banking with his Pierce Avenue neighbor Joseph Noel, recouped his fortunes, and repaid his debts. Soon thereafter, in the 1930s, he murdered his second wife and took his own life. The house was then converted into a rooming house.

Stay on this side of the street and move to:

29. 2142 West Caton Street. Before you is a 14-room mansion and one of the most elegant homes on the street. The workmanship, both inside and out, is highly detailed. A facade of rusticated pink sandstone at street level is transformed into one of textured brick on the upper stories. The turret, with its original spike finial, is supported by a free-standing Romanesque column. The cornice is of pressed metal, and the columns of polished granite. The house always remained a single-family home, and many of the interior fixtures are original, as are the stained-glass windows, the woodwork, and all the hardware.

Crossing the street, walk back to:

30. 2147 West Caton Street. William A. Thoresen commissioned this Classic Revival home, which was completed in 1906. The house is built of flat cut gray stone, and trimmed out entirely in metal. Thoresen, it seems, owned an architectural metals mill, and the products of his factory adorn much of the home's exterior; the interior, as well, is finished in tinwork, to include the domed ceiling in the dining room. The porch also has a tin ceiling, and you should take note of other examples of exterior ornamentation in metal, particularly the garlands of grapes and flowers. On all the homes on the block, only this one has a flat roof.

Next door is:

31. 2145 West Caton Street. Remember John F. Smulski from the "Paderewski" house on Pierce Avenue (see Stop 20, above)? Well, this was his original home, when his father was the first publisher of a Polish-language newspaper in Chicago. Before losing his fortune and his life as a result of the 1929 stock market crash, Smulski too had been a partner with Mr. Noel in the Northwest Savings Bank. He was also a failed Republican candidate in the Chicago mayoral race of 1911.

Retrace your steps along Leavitt Street to North Avenue and turn left. That large complex of buildings at 2150 West North Avenue is:

32. The Association House. Related in spirit to the settlement house tradition, this institution, directed toward combating the effects of chronic poverty on immigrant women, was begun in 1899 by the YWCA. The current building's cornerstone was laid in 1905 by Jane Addams, founder of the settlement house movement. Local businesses assumed financial support of Association House when men were admitted in 1910, and the YWCA chose to leave. Today Association House continues to serve as an emergency shelter, and provides courses in adult education along with a range of other social programs.

From the next intersection, looking north along Hoyne Avenue toward the southeast corner of Concord, that factory-like building you see was once the neighborhood livery stable where locals stored their carriages and boarded their horses. The building, which did become a factory when the horse and buggy went out, has since been converted to condos. The final stop on our tour is at 2039 West North Avenue, a building that until recently housed the:

33. Luxor Baths. An attempt in the 1980s to "yuppify" this old immigrant spa, once a favorite hangout of the Chicago mob according to legend, was not successful. New owners attempted to upgrade the old Russian and Turkish steam baths by adding modern health club amenities. A public bath on this scale is unfortunately no longer feasible, like so many vanishing institutions. The building is an interesting artifact in its own right, and is likely to be preserved, retaining its characteristic shell, while being gutted inside and turned to some other use.

At the next corner, you have returned to the three-road

intersection where the tour began. The tall building across Milwaukee Avenue is the **Northwest Tower Building,** one of the finest examples of art deco design in Chicago, constructed by the downtown architectural firm of Holabird and Root in 1929. At the time the 12-story building opened, it was the tallest structure outside of the downtown area.

REFUELING STOP Right off North Avenue in the shadow of the elevated subway tracks is the **Busy Bee,** 1546 North Damen Avenue (tel. 772-4433), perfect for those who'd like to rest their legs, and maybe have a good simple meal and a cup of coffee. A favorite here is a breakfast plate of eggs, kielbasa, and potatoes. Check out the large photographs of "old" Wicker Park mounted on the walls around the restaurant.

Oak Park

Start: Frank Lloyd Wright Home and Studio, 951 Chicago Avenue, Oak Park (tel. 708/848-1500 for complete tour information).

Public Transportation: The best option is the METRA commuter line. Board the train at the Northwestern station, 500 West Madison Street in downtown Chicago. Get off at the Oak Park/ Marion Street station. The trip takes about 20 minutes. The westbound Lake Street/Dan Ryan elevated train also stops in Oak Park at Harlem Avenue, the end of the line. This line is not considered safe, however, and it will be shut down for at least two years beginning in January 1994 to undergo major repairs.

Finish: Hemingway Birthplace, 339 North Oak Park Avenue.

Time: 2 to 3 hours.

Best Times: If you want to follow this itinerary to the letter, coordinate your start with the times of scheduled tours at the Wright Home and Studio and Unity Temple—the two most important sights in Oak Park. The Home and Studio tour schedule is Monday to Friday at 11am, 1pm, and 3pm; Saturday and Sunday 11am to 4pm. The schedule for visiting Unity Temple is listed below (see Stop 16). Call ahead for additional summer and holiday hours (tel. 708/848-1500). There are no self-guided tours at the Wright Home and Studio; you must purchase a ticket and take a scheduled tour. Try to arrive 15 minutes in advance of the time you've selected; this guided portion of the tour lasts approximately 45 minutes.

Worst Times: Whenever the Wright Home and Studio or Unity Temple aren't open to the public; or when the weather is simply too inclement.

❶ak Park was settled in the early 1830s by a mill owner with the colorful name of Kettlestrings, but the area didn't really begin to develop until after the Chicago Fire of 1871. Today Oak Park Village is a residential suburb of Chicago, but it is proud to remain a separate municipal entity, just outside the city limits, roughly 10 miles from downtown.

Oak Park's most famous native son was Ernest Hemingway, whose birthplace (the home of his maternal grandfather) has been recently converted into a museum. The village is best known, however, as the great showcase of Frank Lloyd Wright's earliest architectural achievements, and contains some two dozen homes and buildings commissioned by his friends and neighbors. Many of these homes are located within Oak Park's historic district, which forms the core of this excursion. The area abounds not only with examples of Wright's Prairie School architecture, but with magnificent works in the Victorian, Stick, and Italianate styles as well, executed by Wright's contemporaries. One of Wright's most celebrated creations, Unity Temple, is also here, a church he designed and built for his own Unitarian congregation.

☕ **REFUELING STOP   Peterson's Ice Cream Empo-rium,** 1100 Chicago Avenue (tel. 708/386-6131), specia-lizes in family dining and a wide selection of desserts; it's a few short blocks from the Home and Studio. If you'd like to start your tour with a pastry and a cup of take-out coffee, Peterson's is the place.

A tour of Oak Park is essentially a tour of Wright's architectural legacy, and should begin at the:

1. Frank Lloyd Wright Home and Studio. Wright grew up in Richland, a Wisconsin farming community where his father was a preacher and his mother taught school. Wright came to Chicago in 1887, and joined the firm of an architect who had once designed two buildings for an uncle who lived in Hyde Park. Later that same year, the young and largely untrained architect began work for Adler and Sullivan as a draftsman. In 1889, Wright married, and Louis Sullivan lent his by-then chief draftsman $5,000 to purchase land in Oak Park to erect a residence. The original "shingle-style" cottage was completed that same year, and modifications and additions were added over a period of two decades.

As the Wrights' family grew, so did their house. At first, the two-story home was relatively small, a few beautifully designed but compact rooms organized around a central fireplace and surrounded by a geometrically shaped veranda and porch that contained seeds of Wright's later Prairie style. Other features, like the wide horizontal window casement dominating the gable facade on the second floor, also prefigure something of the idiom that would characterize Wright's later work.

By 1894, the Wrights had three children (they would have three more over the next nine years) and the family quarters had become cramped. Wright responded by building a spacious two-story addition. On the ground floor, he expanded the kitchen into a large dining room, and relocated the new kitchen and a maid's room at the rear of the house. Above this extension, he built a large, barrel-vaulted playroom for his children, which has been described as "a structural tour de force . . . a gymnasium, kindergarten, concert hall, and theater all in one." Wright's former home office and studio, on the second floor above the entrance, was partitioned into the girls' and boys' dormitories.

By 1898, Wright had relinquished his offices in downtown Chicago, and attached a workshop complex to his home, which included a two-story octagonal studio with a central atrium, a reception area and private office, and a library, also octagonal in shape. By this time, Wright had fully conceptualized the key elements of his Prairie-style architecture, and many of these innovations were incorporated into his spectacular workspace.

To fully appreciate the scope and aesthetic beauty of Wright's accomplishments here, I strongly advise that you take the tour of the interior offered by the organization that today exercises stewardship over this remarkable shrine to the Great American Architect. The Frank Lloyd Wright Home and Studio Foundation, over a 12-year period ending in 1986, oversaw a massive restoration of the Home and Studio, returning it to its general appearance in 1909, when Wright left for Europe with the wife of a client under a cloud of social disapproval.

Wright continued to own the home until 1925, when he sold it and his family finally vacated the premises. By then the complex had undergone many more significant transformations, and it had fallen into a ruinous condition by the time it was purchased for preservation. It was therefore wise to restore the buildings to the way they appeared during the architect's productive tenure here, where within the space of 11 years he completed 125 buildings—over a quarter of his life's work.

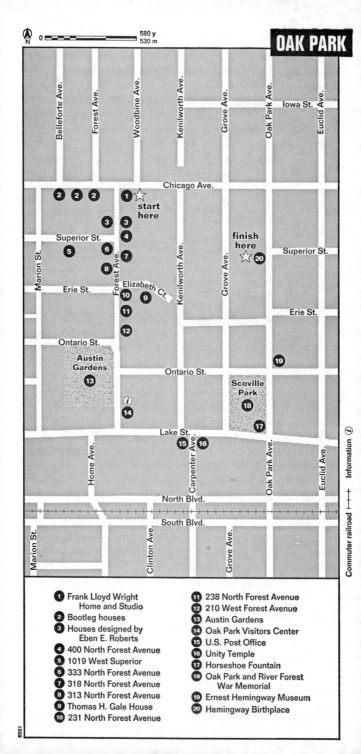

OAK PARK

580 y
530 m

1. Frank Lloyd Wright Home and Studio
2. Bootleg houses
3. Houses designed by Eben E. Roberts
4. 400 North Forest Avenue
5. 1019 West Superior
6. 333 North Forest Avenue
7. 318 North Forest Avenue
8. 313 North Forest Avenue
9. Thomas H. Gale House
10. 231 North Forest Avenue
11. 238 North Forest Avenue
12. 210 West Forest Avenue
13. Austin Gardens
14. Oak Park Visitors Center
15. U.S. Post Office
16. Unity Temple
17. Horseshoe Fountain
18. Oak Park and River Forest War Memorial
19. Ernest Hemingway Museum
20. Hemingway Birthplace

Commuter railroad ┼┼┼┼   Information ⓘ

When you exit the Frank Lloyd Wright Home and Studio, cross Forest Avenue and walk west along Chicago Avenue to the cluster of:

2. bootleg houses. These homes, nos. 1019, 1027, and 1031 Chicago Avenue, were designed and built by Frank Lloyd Wright between 1892 and 1893, while he was still employed by Adler and Sullivan. By the terms of his contract, Wright was not permitted to perform work outside the firm. Sullivan discovered his moonlighting in 1893, causing a permanent rift between the two men, and leading Wright to leave the firm and take up practice on his own. With each of these houses, Wright worked essentially in a Victorian medium that he would ultimately come to despise. Nonetheless, each of these structures already reflects Wright's mastery over those architectural skills that enhanced his cherished vision of simple home comforts.

Return to Forest Avenue and turn right, walking away from Chicago Avenue to:

3. houses designed by Eben E. Roberts. Roberts was another popular Oak Park architect, and a late contemporary of Frank Lloyd Wright's. He designed and executed over 200 houses during his productive career, and worked in every style. No. 426 North Forest Avenue (1897) is a Roberts house following the popular Queen Anne style. With 422 North Forest Avenue (1900), Roberts began to break with the Victorian tradition and pioneer the low, boxy configuration that would characterize many of his later houses. Roberts's own experiment with the idiom of the Prairie School is visible in another of his Forest Avenue homes, no. 415.

Our first sample of Wright's architecture on this block is:

4. 400 North Forest Avenue. This house, built for Dr. William H. Copeland in 1894, is by no means typical of Wright's work in Oak Park. Perhaps the good doctor had ideas of his own, and the young architect simply chose to accommodate him. The house, however, does possess that unmistakable "horizontality" of the Prairie School architecture.

To see E. E. Roberts's own home, take a brief digression west, along the north side of Superior, the first cross street, to:

5. 1019 West Superior. Roberts's home (1911) is remarkable for its lack of pretense in a neighborhood where architectural oneupsmanship was obviously a fashion of the times. If anything, the house appears as a pattern for the cookie-cutter homes of the professional classes that proliferated in suburbs throughout the country after World War II.

Return to Forest Avenue and walk to:

6. 333 North Forest Avenue. This Frank Lloyd Wright creation was built in 1895 for Nathan G. Moore, who enjoined the architect to "give me something Elizabethan." Wright, to be sure, was almost as ambivalent about this Tudor styling as he was about the nonfunctional excesses of ornamentation that he associated with anything in the Victorian mode. Commenting late in life in his memoirs, he wryly noted that "anyone could get a rise out of me by admiring that essay in English half-timber. They all liked it, and I could have gone on unnaturally building them for the rest of my natural life." In 1923, when a devastating fire burned the house down to its first story, Wright was asked to supervise the remodeling. The second time around, Wright departed from the original Tudor genre, adding such spectacular details as the Gothic bay, the cantilevered porch roof, and the Mayan trim.

The visual fare begins to improve exponentially with our next stopping point:

7. 318 North Forest Avenue. The Arthur B. Heurtley House (1902) is something of a fine first draft for Robie House, the Hyde Park home Wright would complete seven years later, and which today is viewed as his residential masterpiece. Certainly to the lay observer, these two homes have much in common. They are both long and low, with walls of richly decorated horizontal windows. Each lies partially hidden behind a brick wall, which in the case of the Heurtley House, rises almost to the roofline, allowing a seemingly narrow space on the second story for a band of glass running the length of the eves. The effect is of a highly stylized battlement lined with glittering gunports. The front door, beneath a very formal archway, remains hidden from view, to suggest both the sanctity of domestic privacy and the illusion of entering one's residence, not directly into the static parlor, but by way of the door yard, the normal place for comings and goings in an active home. This hidden entryway, borrowed from the work of H. R. Richardson by way of Louis Sullivan, would become a trademark of Wright's architecture as well.

Next we come to:

8. 313 North Forest Avenue. Here's a house that pre-dates Wright's arrival in Oak Park by several years, but which he was called upon by Nathan G. Moore to remodel between 1900 and 1906. Moore bought this originally stick style frame house for his daughter, Mary. The house was moved from its foundation on the lot, and turned 90 degrees so its broad front would face Forest Avenue. Wright's remodeling was so radical that little of the appearance of the original house remains. One of the structure's most striking features is the pagoda roof, echoed in the caps over the porch and the third-story dormer. That little building in the yard began its life as a ticket booth at Chicago's 1893 World's Columbia Exhibition.

Here we will make another brief detour, turning left onto Elizabeth Court, the only curved street in Oak Park, to the:

9. Thomas H. Gale House. This 1909 construction at 6 Elizabeth Court has that quintessential Frank Lloyd Wright look. It is in fact a forerunner to Fallingwater, the home Wright built in Bear Run, Pennsylvania, one major source of the narrow image the world in general has of the architect's legacy (another being New York City's somewhat grotesque and surrealistic Guggenheim Museum). Seen as a singular creation without reference to the Wright stereotype, especially here in Oak Park where so many neighboring homes have that doily-like look of respectability, this house provides a pleasant jolt to the visual senses. The double porches, for example, project something latently aggressive, as if a ship's conning tower were ready to bear down upon you but for the fact that its superstructure and hull have been sunk beneath the level of the street.

Return now to Forest Avenue and pause before one of the oldest houses in the village:

10. 231 North Forest Avenue. This is the pattern of Oak Park's earliest dwellings, built circa 1873. Often, cottages like this were remodeled to the point where the simplicity of the original design was completely transformed in the renovation. Others were simply moved to neighborhoods where the real estate was less pricey.

A case in point of a modest cottage being remodeled beyond recognition is:

11. 238 North Forest Avenue, known as the Beachy House. One of Wright's sisters also lived here during the 1930s and 1940s. Like the home at 333 North Forest Avenue, this example of Wright and company's handiwork has the look of a big box at its core to which various surface forms have been added to soften the structure's square-like symmetry. Four different materials—limestone, brick, plaster, and wood trim—were used to lend depth and texture to the facade. Notice that the lot this house sits on is unusually deep.

A few steps down the block is:

12. 210 West Forest Avenue. Here at the Frank W. Thomas House, we return again to the horizontal layout that has rendered such pleasant results in the hands of the master modernist, who saw in this form an affirmation of the human link to nature. This 1901 construction is considered Wright's first contribution to the Prairie School of architecture, despite the fact that he had by then already built a house with similar dimensions in his home state of Wisconsin. Some of the features characteristic of Prairie architecture found in the Thomas House are the flat, hip roof—used to eliminate wasted attic space—and the small windows on the second floor, which in this instance suggest a Chinese influence. Also the house has no basement, which Wright came to consider "unwholesome." Here Wright also employed the shielded entryway; the rounded portal appears to shelter a front door, but instead only leads to one at the top of a concealed stairway.

Across the street from the Thomas House is:

13. **Austin Gardens.** This attractive green space is named for one of Oak Park's original teetotaling settlers, Henry W. Austin. For the most part, it should be noted, Oak Park remains "dry" to this day, though village statutes were modified to allow the service of alcoholic beverages in several local restaurants. Note the bust of Frank Lloyd Wright at the Forest Avenue entrance to the park.

Beyond the park, on the left before you get to Lake Street, at 158 Forest Avenue, is the:

14. **Oak Park Visitors Center** (tel. 708/848-1500). Any questions about local orientation can be answered here. There are clean restrooms, and various items for sale, including maps, guidebooks, postcards, and tour tickets. Adjacent to the facility is a parking lot. The center is open daily from 10am to 5pm.

Continue to Lake Street, turn left, and cross the street. At the side entrance nearest you, go inside the:

15. **U.S. Post Office.** This is one of those massive public buildings worth examining more closely for several reasons. For one, the deco interior is beautifully appointed and impeccably maintained. There are several murals in the romantic Americana vein, and the wrought iron grillwork surrounding the portals is an amusing tableau of figures and vehicles used over the years for mail delivery.

Exit the post office at the far end of the building onto Kenilworth Avenue. Across the street at 875 Lake Street is a National Historic Landmark building that many consider Frank Lloyd Wright's most perfect creation. If you have a camera with you, the best place to frame the Unity Temple is from the rear steps of the post office. So take your pictures before crossing over to:

16. **Unity Temple.** "The reality of the building," said Wright, "is the space within." Nowhere perhaps is this more true in this architect's work than with this extraordinarily unconventional house of worship. Called upon by his congregation to replace their old church, which had burned to the ground, Wright submitted his plan for the "temple" in 1905.

His choice of concrete for the structure was pragmatic;

building materials had to be selected with an eye toward economy, given the limited funds available for the project. It is not surprising, therefore, that to one's initial, cursory examination, this massive block of concrete may seem offputting—even ugly. But a closer look will reveal that the exterior, too, of Wright's "little jewel" is not without its grace in either form or detail. The outline of the building, especially when viewed from the side, is a sight of rare structural beauty. And much of the decorative detail serves some functional purpose as well: The hollow columns contain the original heating ducts, the roof's waffle construction allows the infiltration of natural light, and so forth.

The interior of the temple, however, within the actual chapel, is where Wright delivers his knockout blow simultaneously to the mind's eye and the aesthetic senses. Here Wright, in his lifelong crusade against Victorian sentimentality, offers the most convincing evidence that beauty is not synonymous with cuteness, no matter how complex in appearance. The lines, the forms, the colors, the composition within this singular space could not be more spare and restrained. And yet the effect is monumental, a tribute to the transcendental deism of Thoreau and Emerson. Here one does not bow before the supernatural, but stands erect with full confidence in the human spirit and all its unfulfilled potential. Wright himself was well aware from the beginning of how daring a statement was articulated by this work; he also felt considerable apprehension, and failed to attend the inaugural service, not at all certain of how his fellow congregants would react.

You will need a ticket to enter Unity Temple, and may choose an accompanied or self-guided tour, depending on the day of your visit. In either case, expert docents will provide a suitably detailed account of each architectural twist and turn Wright employed within the church. Unity Temple is open Monday to Friday from 1 to 4pm for self-guided tours, and Saturday and Sunday at 2pm for guided tours.

Cross Lake Street, follow it past Grove Avenue, and enter Scoville Park. At the southeast corner of the park is:

17. Horseshoe Fountain. This park adornment was designed by Frank Lloyd Wright in 1909.

Now walk toward the center of the park until you come to the:

18. Oak Park and River Forest War Memorial. This monument was erected in 1925 in tribute to World War I servicemen from surrounding communities. On the southeast side of the base, you will see the name of Ernest Hemingway.

Continue diagonally through the park until reaching Oak

Park Avenue at Ontario Street. At 200 North Oak Park Avenue, you may wish to pay a brief visit to the:

19. Ernest Hemingway Museum (tel. 708/848-2222). Oak Park has only recently begun to rally around the memory of its Nobel and Pulitzer prize–winning native son, Ernest Hemingway. A portion of the ground floor of this former church, now the Oak Park Arts Center, is given over to a small but interesting display of Hemingway memorabilia. There is also a six-minute video presentation that sheds considerable light on Hemingway's time in Oak Park, where he spent the first 18 years of his life; it's particularly good on the writer's high school experiences. The museum's hours are limited: Wednesday and Sunday from 1 to 5pm, and Saturday from 10am to 5pm; there is an admission fee.

To see where Hemingway was born, continue up the block to 339 North Oak Park Avenue, the:

20. Hemingway Birthplace. On July 21, 1899, in the home of his maternal grandparents, the author of several great American novels was born. The home was purchased recently by a local foundation to serve as a museum; it has been restored to reflect its appearance during Hemingway's boyhood. Hemingway's actual boyhood home, still privately owned, is located several blocks from here, not far from the Wright Home and Studio, at 600 North Kenilworth Avenue. The hours at the Hemingway Birthplace museum are the same as those at the Hemingway Museum above. A special admission price covers both museums.

Our tour of Oak Park ends here. You may easily walk back to the train station along Lake Street, or take a break before returning to Chicago at any one of several restaurants on Oak Park Avenue.

REFUELING STOP   The eateries on this block offer a variety of cuisines. If you want to keep it simple, try **Erik's Delicatessen,** 107 North Oak Park Avenue (tel. 708/848-8805), where sandwiches and a salad bar top the menu.

The Magnificent Mile

Start: Michigan Avenue Bridge.

Public Transportation: Take the Howard line to Roosevelt Avenue, or the Michigan Avenue bus to the vicinity of the Chicago River.

Finish: The Drake Hotel.

Time: 1½ to 2 hours; longer if you browse heavily or shop along the way.

Best Times: During normal business hours, seven days a week. Check shops for closing times; many of the vertical malls are open nightly till 8pm or later, except Sundays. Between Thanksgiving and Christmas, the special lighting makes the Magnificent Mile a special place to walk after dark as well.

Worst Times: Whenever the shops or malls are closed.

No section of Chicago reflects the driving changes of the 20th century more than this strip of Michigan Avenue between the Chicago River and Oak Street Beach known as the Magnificent Mile. While the original settlement of Chicago actually began on the neighborhood's periphery, on the banks of the Chicago River, commercial development within the city for many years spread toward the south.

Of course, most of the earlier 19th-century construction in what is today River North, the North Michigan Avenue area (including

Streeterville), the Gold Coast, and Lincoln Park as far north as Fullerton Avenue did not survive the Chicago Fire. Between 1871 and the mid-1920s, the vast tracts covering these contiguous neighborhoods were indistinguishable from the other outlying areas surrounding the downtown Loop. And what is today the North Michigan Avenue area was even a bit more shabby than most because of its concentration of cheaply constructed "fire shanties," as much of the temporary post-fire housing was dubbed. True, the more daring elements among the city's Mandarin merchant class began to build their mansions in the River North neighborhood, and along the newly laid out Lake Shore Drive in the 1880s. But between those pockets of isolated splendor, and the river bordering downtown, North Michigan Avenue (then called Pine Street) had more the look of frontier than metropolis well into the 20th century.

Indeed, the very dimensions of the landmass along the lakefront were substantially smaller than they are today. Tons of rubble from the ruins of the fire, plus excess fill from myriad post-fire construction sites transformed acres of watery frontage east of Pine Street into valuable real estate. Gradually, the area's aspect began to change, but that large spurt of energy required for full-blown development was slow to materialize despite the fact that Daniel Burnham's 1909 Plan of Chicago had laid the conceptual groundwork for creating a wide boulevard to replace Pine Street. It was not until the 1920s, however, that the engines of urban expansion were sufficiently fired and the first tentative steps could be taken to realize Burnham's vision. The rest, as they say, is history.

Our tour of North Michigan Avenue—the Magnificent Mile—begins on the opposite bank of the Chicago River, across the:

1. **Michigan Avenue Bridge.** Development of the near north side awaited the construction of a bridge in this location, linking Michigan Avenue below the river to its new extension above. In 1920, the deed was done. The site anchoring the southern end of the bridge is of deep historical significance to the city. Here, in 1803, Fort Dearborn was erected; at that time it was a major military garrison at the threshold of the Northwest Territory, an area just then opening up to settlement by restless citizens from the old, established eastern colonies of the new republic. An outline of the original fort is marked on the roadway and in the sidewalk.

There are several other attractions of interest on this bridge. Don't miss the decorative relief sculptures adorning the pylons, *Defence and Regeneration* by Henry Hering to the north, and *The Discoverers and The Pioneers* by James Earle Fraser to the south. Like all the spans across the river in downtown Chicago, this is a movable bridge that must open frequently to accommodate a still considerable amount of water traffic below. The vista from the Michigan Avenue Bridge is particularly fine, taking in a fair stretch of the river skyline to its west—one of the prettiest sights in the city—and opening to a wide view of the lake to its east. The river esplanade you see on the northern bank will run all the way to Navy Pier at the end of Grand Street; its completion is projected for 1995.

Cross the bridge and stop just beyond the northern end. The very distinctive building standing on the west side of the street, a fitting and monumental gateway to a grand boulevard, is 400 North Michigan Avenue, the:

2. William Wrigley, Jr., Building. When this building went up—actually two buildings side by side—between 1919 and 1924, a trend began in Chicago to match the ever-rising altitude of the New York skyline. The Wrigley family of chewing gum (and Chicago Cubs) fame continues to own and operate this imposing building, which glitters brightly in the sunlight, owing to the white terra-cotta cladding covering its facade. In fact, six shades of white distinguish these surface tiles; the darkest tone begins at the base, and the colors gradually lighten as the sheathing rises to the roofline. That same brightness is reflected beautifully in the water of the nearby river, and is highlighted by night in the glow of innumerable flood lights.

In this same location, on the east side of the street, behind the sweeping plaza known as Pioneer Court, is 401 North Michigan Avenue, the:

3. Equitable Building. When this great slab went up in 1965, Mies van der Rohe was still the rage among urban architects. As a result there are many skyscrapers in Chicago that derive their inspiration from the philosophy of pure functionalism that was promoted by the onetime Bauhaus innovator in his later years. What makes this otherwise overpowering computer chip of a structure less obtrusive in this prized riverside setting is the fact that the Tribune Company, which resides in the landmark building next door, stipulated that the deep set-back with its wide front yard be used as public space when they agreed to part with the property. Part of the plaza's charm is the way it wraps around the building, and even leads to a stairway that descends to river level. A block to the east behind the Equitable Building are two of Chicago's newest large-scale extravaganzas, facing each other from opposing corners on Columbia Avenue: the NBC tower, designed to look like a building from the 1930s, and the Sheraton Chicago Hotel and Towers, a first-class convention establishment.

Walk behind the Equitable Building through the plaza on the north side of the building to the overlook above:

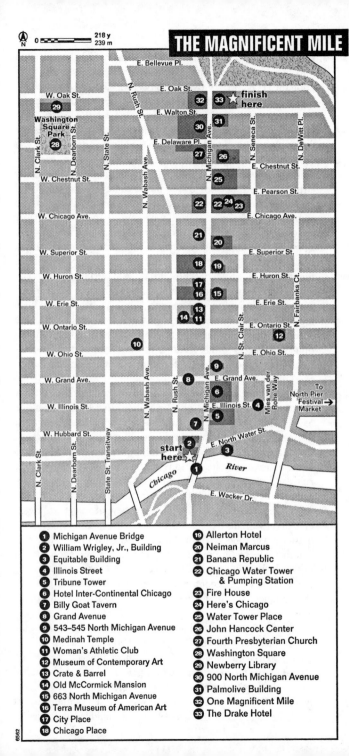

THE MAGNIFICENT MILE

1. Michigan Avenue Bridge
2. William Wrigley, Jr., Building
3. Equitable Building
4. Illinois Street
5. Tribune Tower
6. Hotel Inter-Continental Chicago
7. Billy Goat Tavern
8. Grand Avenue
9. 543–545 North Michigan Avenue
10. Medinah Temple
11. Woman's Athletic Club
12. Museum of Contemporary Art
13. Crate & Barrel
14. Old McCormick Mansion
15. 663 North Michigan Avenue
16. Terra Museum of American Art
17. City Place
18. Chicago Place
19. Allerton Hotel
20. Neiman Marcus
21. Banana Republic
22. Chicago Water Tower & Pumping Station
23. Fire House
24. Here's Chicago
25. Water Tower Place
26. John Hancock Center
27. Fourth Presbyterian Church
28. Washington Square
29. Newberry Library
30. 900 North Michigan Avenue
31. Palmolive Building
32. One Magnificent Mile
33. The Drake Hotel

4. **Illinois Street.** From this vantage point, which was planned into the area's development as a public amenity, you can gaze upon the great corridor fronting City Front Center. Down below, accessible by stairs, is Illinois Street, which leads to the entertainment complex known as the North Pier Festival Market.

Back on the boulevard, the grand tower that completes the framing of this postcard composition, which has become a visual signature of Chicago, is 435 North Michigan Avenue, the:

5. **Tribune Tower.** This is truly one of Chicago's most interesting structures, both because of the way it came into existence, and for a particularly unique feature that adorns its exterior. The Trib wanted to celebrate its 25th anniversary in style, so the paper announced a contest. They asked for submissions of designs for a new building, and they pledged to build the winning design. Needless to say, all the top contenders in the country weighed in for this one; world-class architects vied against world-class architects. Walter Gropius and Eliel Saarinen—the runner-up—were among the contestants. In all, 264 entries were received, reflecting the entire alphabet of possibilities for the modern skyscraper that were then being considered by contemporary architects (though, naturally, most derived their inspirations from various classical forms of the more or less distant past).

The winner, a study in Gothic, was drawn—and ultimately constructed—by the firm of John Meade Howells and Raymond M. Hood. The tower stands 36 stories tall, and is most distinguished by the sculptured upper stories, which suggest something of the medieval cathedral. Imbedded at various points in the exterior wall are the souvenir bits and pieces of historical ruins and monuments, with all origins duly labeled. These were gathered by the Tribune's founder and its ruling tyrant for many years, Col. Robert R. McCormick, nephew of the great "Reaper"; along with his trusty international correspondents, he was a master grave robber of the world's most treasured antiquities. Another cute feature ornamenting the Trib Tower is the manner in which the two principal architects signed their work. Among the stone carvings decorating a three-story arch which surrounds the entrance, are the figures of Robin Hood and a "howling" dog.

Another historical building joining this impressive ensemble at the beginning of the Magnificent Mile lies across Illinois Street, 505 North Michigan Avenue, today housing the:

6. **Hotel Inter-Continental Chicago.** This old duck helped ring in the Depression when it was completed in 1929. Originally, the Medinah Athletic Club was housed within its art moderne interior. In the late 1980s, the building underwent a

massive renovation while being converted into the first-class accommodations of the Hotel Inter-Continental Chicago. The building boasts elaborately decorated relief panels on three sides of the facade exterior. Take a quick do-si-do around the lobby for a study in grandeur, albeit in miniature.

Cross Michigan Avenue, which you will notice is elevated at this point. Backtrack to the north end of the Wrigley Building, where a stairwell descends to the subterranean Hubbard Street. In the shadowy crevice beneath the concrete walkway at the bottom of the stairs is the:

7. Billy Goat Tavern. This short-order dive and tap room is a hangout for newspaper workers from the nearby offices of both the *Chicago Tribune* and the *Chicago Sun Times*. The official address is 430 North Michigan Avenue. This was the place John Belushi parodied in his classic skit on *Saturday Night Live,* a moment in the life of a crabby Greek short-order cook. The Billy Goat, incidentally, has a cheap and popular breakfast special, available on weekdays only.

Return to Michigan Avenue and walk to:

8. Grand Avenue, which eventually leads to Navy Pier, about a half mile due east. After 1995, Navy Pier will have been completely transformed from an on-again, off-again exhibition and open-air market space into a veritable Tivoli Gardens by the Lake. When the gigantic redevelopment plan is completed, Navy Pier will offer visitors the following attractions: a four-acre park for fairs, events, and performances; a waterside Farmer's Market with arts and crafts and fresh produce for sale in season; a Family Pavilion, which will house the Chicago Children's Museum, a new IMAX theatre, and a six-story indoor park and atrium called the Crystal Gardens, plus an exciting mix of shops and restaurants; and an enormous new exhibition hall of 170,000 square feet.

Between Grand and Ohio on the east side of the avenue is:

9. 543–545 North Michigan Avenue. This mildly deco building provides a more accurate profile of the scale of Michigan Avenue as it appeared during the 1920s than do the Wrigley Building or the Tribune Tower, whose verticality was an exception, paying homage more to Manhattan than Chicago, where canyonization was a choice, not a necessity. The building's mansard roof reflects the French training of architect Phillip B. Maher, and the reliefs of the female nudes above the entry recall the days when a salon d'haute couture occupied the original storefront.

A slight digression two blocks west along Ohio Street to 600 North Wabash may be of interest, to see the:

10. Medinah Temple. This fanciful Moorish palace is the regional headquarters of the Shriners, and site of their annual—and highly regarded—circus, usually scheduled over a three-week period in late February and early March. Ohio Street is also a gateway to the culinary wonderland that has sprung up in recent years throughout River North, the neighborhood immediately east of the Magnificent Mile. (See *Frommer's Chicago* for a full listing of these restaurants.)

As we continue up Michigan Avenue, the next four cross streets we encounter above Ohio Street are named for the Great Lakes. On the corner of Ontario Street at 626 North Michigan Avenue is the:

11. Woman's Athletic Club. The style and grace of this Phillip B. Maher creation, built in 1928, is reminiscent of an entire era of transatlantic steamship lines, and "putting on the Ritz." You can almost imagine this building having been imported stone by stone directly from Paris, where its many models and predecessors reside to this day.

A block and a half east at 237 East Ontario Street, between St. Clair and Fairbanks, is the:

12. Museum of Contemporary Art. This is the museum's old location—or it will be after 1995, if the construction of its new home (which we'll pass further along on this itinerary at Stop 23) is completed according to plan. The museum has an unusual and wide collection of artworks in video, laser, and electronic forms.

Now return to Michigan Avenue and head north to the corner of Erie Street. At 646 North Michigan Avenue is:

13. Crate & Barrel. In the view of local promoters, this attractive, ultra-modern retail space represents the wave of future development along the Magnificent Mile, an updated incarnation of the scale and elegance of the late 1920s when three-, four-, and five-story buildings dominated the immediate skyline. Householders beware: There's some mighty attractive "stuff" in this store.

By walking west on Erie Street for a block or two, you can get some notion of what Old River North looked like on the periphery of Pine Street during the 1880s, when the wealthy built mansions on the ruins of immigrant houses after the Great Fire. First is the:

14. Old McCormick Mansion. The entrance is on North Rush Street at no. 660. This old manse (1875) belonged to Cyrus McCormick's brother, and is one of several residences of the clan remaining from when this area was known as McCormickville. Behind the roofline of an addition that today houses Lawry's restaurant, at 631 North Rush Street, you can make out a fragment of the splendid palazzo that belonged to L.

Hamilton McCormick, another family beneficiary of Cyrus's good fortune.

On the next corner at State is 40 East Erie Street, also a mansion of the period, the former home (1883) of one Samuel M. Nickerson, and today the R. H. Love Galleries.

Back on Michigan Avenue, turn your attention to:

15. 663 North Michigan Avenue. This building has been referred to as the most successful retail space in the city of Chicago. Two flagship shops occupy the ground floor, Nike and Sony. Both need to be entered to be appreciated for their innovations in interior decor and layout. The Nike store is a three-story pavilion, divided into various sports environments, and seems very much a vision of the retail environment of the 21st century. The Sony store is less glitzy, and is really more of a hands-on showcase than an outlet for the endless stream of electronic gadgets from Japan, where generations of technological change are measured in months, not years.

At 666 North Michigan Avenue, the home of one of the more interesting art collections in the city, is the:

16. Terra Museum of American Art. The focus is Native work created in the 18th, 19th, and 20th centuries. What began as the private collection of industrialist Daniel J. Terra now comprises an inventory of over 400 unique pieces spread over many galleries.

One of the more visually daring structures among Chicago's most recent crop of skyscrapers is at 676 North Michigan Avenue:

17. City Place, built in 1990. The curvy, futuristic design running the height of the facade looks like the upright panel of a giant pinball machine; you'll either find it very attractive, if you like that sort of thing (I do), or, as one critic remarked, "garish." The middle floors of the multi-use high-rise are occupied by the Omni Hotel Chicago. At ground level is the Stuart Brent Bookstore, where the owner of the same name has installed his adaptation of a bibliophile's paradise.

Across Huron Street is another behemoth, 700 North Michigan Avenue, or:

18. Chicago Place. Saks Fifth Avenue is the flagship of this, Chicago's most recently inaugurated retail skyscraper (1991). Some 80 shops and stores, wrapped around an atrium, rise eight stories from street level, to an informal café bathed in natural light and surrounded by potted greenery.

Directly across Michigan Avenue from Chicago Place, with its entrance at 140 East Huron Street, is the:

19. Allerton Hotel. This 1924 vintage building is a rare find along the Magnificent Mile, a reasonably comfortable hotel where you can find a room—at least on weekends—for less than $100 a night. The rooms are large and well kept, but not fashionable; the Allerton does a fair business with tourists from the heartland who arrive in Chicago on chartered buses.

The spirit of Texan exaggeration animates our next stop at 737 North Michigan Avenue—it's the First Church of Upward Mobility, otherwise known as:

20. Neiman Marcus. The four-story lobby, trimmed in marble and brass, and made plush by every imaginable item of conspicuous consumption and architectural excess, would have brought a blush to the cheeks of a Roman emperor. As commercial theatre at its most fantastic, no one does it on a grander scale. Definitely worth a digression for a few moments of gawking and jaw dropping. This multi-use complex—the store (1983) and the high-altitude Olympia Center (1986) around the corner at 161 East Chicago—are the work of Skidmore, Owings & Merrill, and pay homage in a variety of design and decorative features to the styles of Louis Sullivan and H. H. Richardson.

In keeping with the retail theme-park fantasy of our last attraction, check out this Chicago outlet of the by-now familiar outfitter of off-the-road globetrotting, at 744 North Michigan Avenue:

21. Banana Republic. If "the medium is the message," then merely stepping through the threshold of this ersatz tropical longhouse will transport you instantly to Bali, decked out in a wardrobe of khaki and cotton in the best tradition of Indiana Jones. The remodeling of the building's exterior in 1991 followed the design of Robert A. M. Stern.

Across Chicago Avenue, on both sides of Michigan Avenue, are two structures that lay claim, without dispute, to the status of First Landmark of Chicago, the:

22. Chicago Water Tower & Pumping Station. Two years after their construction in 1869, the path of the Chicago Fire swept away virtually every building in the vicinity. But the Water Tower and Pumping Station survived unscathed. Fate decrees its choices with a certain irony; why, many wags have wondered over the years, was so much surrounding beauty reduced to ashes while these two beasts were allowed to stand? One wit suggested that both buildings look like they belong at the bottom of a fish tank, and indeed they do appear for all the world like mutant sand castles left behind from the set of some made-for-TV sci-fi melodrama. The most unkind notice the Water Tower ever received was from modernism's High Priest of Beauty himself. Oscar Wilde, touring America in 1881, dismissed it categorically as a "monstrosity."

The castellated style, here practiced by the accomplished

Chicago architect William W. Boyington in the medium of yellow tinted Illinois limestone, was, however, wildly popular in its day. And, of course, whatever one's aesthetic judgement about the value of the architecture—on three occasions in the past 90 years, the tower narrowly escaped demolition—the Water Tower's importance as a symbol of Chicago's survival cannot be underestimated. A restoration campaign begun in 1962 finally gave public recognition to that fact. An information booth, staffed by the Chicago Office of Tourism, is also on the premises.

Turn right and walk east on Chicago Avenue. At no. 202 East, notice the:

23. **Fire House.** This is one of the oldest stations in the city, operating since 1903, and built in imitation of the castellated Gothic style of the Water Tower & Pumping Station. Tiny Seneca Park with its Eli Schulman Playground surrounds the fire station. Across the small street, named for Mies van der Rohe, is the future site of the Chicago Museum of Contemporary Art, scheduled for completion in 1995. Eli Schulman, incidentally, was a Chicago restaurateur and philanthropist whose famous steak house, Eli's, is just across the street.

REFUELING STOP Eli's . . . The Place for Steak, 215 East Chicago Avenue (tel. 642-1393), is famous for its cheesecakes, making the restaurant the perfect spot for a mid-morning or mid-afternoon coffee break. There are 50 varieties of cheesecake from which to choose (author's choice: the pumpkin).

Now cross over to Pearson Street along Mies van der Rohe Way. The palazzo on the northeast corner of the intersection was the residence of the renowned architect for whom the street is named. Mies, according to local lore, had free digs in the complex he designed on nearby Lake Shore Drive, but had to flee because every time the tenants had a maintenance problem, they called on the architect, as if he were the building's super.

Turn left on Pearson Street, and walk back toward Michigan Avenue. Here on Pearson Street, in the Pumping Station, is the entrance to:

24. **Here's Chicago,** an introduction to the city's past and present in the form of a multimedia tourist show.

The massive, block-sized building between Pearson Street and Chestnut, directly across from the Pumping Station at 845 North Michigan Avenue, is:

25. Water Tower Place. This is the dean of Chicago's vertical malls, built in 1976. When Marshall Field and Company, Chicago's most popular homegrown department store, opened this "uptown" branch, many city denizens no longer had a reason to visit State Street, the traditional center of retailing in the Loop, where the original Marshall Field's remains in place. Among the other high-toned occupants of Water Tower Place are Lord & Taylor and the 431-room Ritz Carlton Hotel, spread over 22 floors.

REFUELING STOP Richard Melman, Chicago's magician of pop eateries, has done it again. If it's variety you want—a selection of platters and snack foods from home and abroad, served up from a dozen different stands, carnival-style—then check out **Food Life** (tel. 335-FOOD), on the mezzanine level of Water Tower Place.

On the next block north at 875 North Michigan Avenue stands a 100-story building that is only the third-tallest structure in Chicagoland, the:

26. John Hancock Center. "Big John" (1969) was the first real giant to appear on the Chicago skyline, setting a trend toward high-altitude construction in downtown Chicago that only began to wane in the early 1990s, as developers predicted a return to the small-scale buildings that were once so characteristic of North Michigan Avenue. New Yorkers in particular were outraged when Chicago dared to raise a building that eclipsed their much-revered Empire State, for so many years the tallest building in the world. But "Big John's" claim to that distinction was short lived, as construction companies in Chicago, Toronto, and New York, began a game of skyrise oneupsmanship.

In Chicago, however, "Big John" has not been forgotten; among architects and engineers in particular, the building retains a strong following. The techheads speak highly of the building's structural innovations, the crisscross steel framing, the tapering form that suggests a monument of super proportions, and the neat little fact that certain engineering breakthroughs kept the cost down to that of a building half its height. An observatory on the 94th floor is open to the public, as is a bar and restaurant duplex between the 95th and 96th floors.

Across from "Big John" at 866 North Michigan Avenue is:

27. Fourth Presbyterian Church (1914). The iconoclasm historically associated with the preachings of Knox and Calvin takes a back seat when the congregation in question caters to the spiritual needs of the well-to-do. This splendid creation in

STREETERVILLE

The area around the John Hancock Center, east to the Lake and north to Oak Street, bordering North Michigan Avenue, is known as Streeterville. Behind this colorful name is a colorful tale. In 1886, George Wellington "Cap" Streeter, a circus showman, ran his leaky scow aground in the shallows near what is today Chicago Avenue. When, after several weeks, the tides refused to free the stranded craft, Cap Streeter dug in for the duration. First he built a narrow causeway, spanning the swampy wetland between his boat and the shoreline. Next, he invited local builders to dump their fill near his involuntary abode.

Within a short time, Streeter was surrounded by 150 acres of prime real estate in a neighborhood undergoing a period of rapid development. Since this landmass did not appear on the map of the Illinois shoreline survey, Streeter claimed it for the federal government, and appointed himself as territorial governor. When Streeter started trying to sell off his holdings, the city of Chicago finally tired of the antics of the man the local papers dubbed the "Squatter King." Streeter was taken to court, but it was not until 1918 that an order was issued for his eviction—and not for squatting on city land, but for violating the municipal blue laws by selling spirits on Sundays. Cap Streeter's tenancy in his landfill "federal district" had lasted over 20 years, and it is only fitting that today the area he helped create should bear his name.

Gothic by Ralph Adams Cram and Howard Van Doren Shaw—the latter a parishioner—complete with its cloistered courtyard, illuminated ceiling, and saintly statuary, is much closer to the Roman tradition than to the plain-wrapper meeting houses favored by more simple folk since the days of the Reformation.

A brief detour off the Magnificent Mile, several blocks to the west along Delaware to Dearborn, is recommended here for those who would like to visit the oldest park in Chicago:

28. **Washington Square.** This is Chicago's famous Bughouse Square, which I first read about in the Studs Lonigan trilogy of James T. Farrell. In this "outdoor forum of garrulous hobohemia," an oddball collection of soap-box orators, expounding on anything from free love to a stateless society, used to harangue each other and crowds of derisive, delighted onlookers throughout the 1920s.

Surrounding Washington Square are some fine old mansions and renovated town houses, and across the street at 60 West Walton Street, is the glorious:

29. Newberry Library. The Newberry was established in 1887, and has been a researcher's paradise ever since, particularly for those involved with European and American studies. Included in the collection are many rare volumes, over five million manuscripts, and 60,000 maps; many interesting artifacts are also on display. The institution was the bequest of Chicago financier and merchant Walter Loomis Newberry, and the building the work of architect Henry Ives Cobb.

Return to Michigan Avenue along Walton Street. On the southwest corner is:

30. 900 North Michigan Avenue. There is something slightly sinister about the design of this building, with its cold, monumental beauty—an unconscious echo of the work of Albert Speer, Hitler's favorite architect. Locally, 900 North Michigan is known as the Bloomingdale's Building; it's unlikely that the arrival of any franchise in Chicago was ever greeted with the degree of fanfare and fawning that accompanied the installation of Bloomies. That event, ironically, coincided with the very period when this giant arbiter of yuppie fashions was undergoing a state of near financial collapse. Like its three principal competitors among the Magnificent Mile's vertical shopping malls, 900 North Michigan is crammed with fine specialty shops and, like Chicago Place, they surround an atrium eight stories high.

For the last three points of interest, we will crisscross Michigan Avenue several times. Directly across from Bloomies at 919 North Michigan Avenue is the original:

31. Palmolive Building. But for years this 1929 vintage study in deco was called the Playboy Building, during the era when the skin-mag giant ruled its empire from Chicago.

Crossing again, the building at 940–980 North Michigan Avenue on the corner of Oak Street is known as:

32. One Magnificent Mile. A main attraction here is the presence of Spiaggia, one of Chicago's most consistently popular Italian restaurants since the mid-1980s.

Our tour of North Michigan Avenue appropriately draws to a close at the building across from One Magnificent Mile, with its entrance at 140 East Walton Street:

33. The Drake Hotel. Built in 1920 by Marshall & Fox, the Drake has maintained a consistent level of fine service and luxury accommodations for over 70 years. The 13-story building is a Chicago landmark, constructed of Bedford limestone in a design inspired by the Italian palaces of the late Renaissance. A stroll through the lobby, especially the serene and tasteful Palm Court, is definitely worthwhile. With its privileged view of the lakefront, the Drake stands at the transition point between downtown Chicago and the elegant residential neighborhood called the Gold Coast.

The Gold Coast

Start: East Lake Shore Drive, across from the Oak Street Beach (behind the Drake Hotel).
Public Transportation: Your best bet is the Michigan Avenue bus; get off between Walton and Oak streets.
Finish: Bellevue Place and Michigan Avenue.
Time: 2 hours.
Best Times: Before or after the morning rush on weekdays when the streets are empty enough to enjoy unjostled solitude, but sufficiently early on a bright day when the sun is low in the sky and casts flat and even light. Sunday is the ideal day for this walk anytime of year.
Worst Times: Whenever crowded beach or streets could make the walk heavy going.

The Gold Coast is the silk-stocking district of Chicago. Its confines are small and exclusive as you might imagine of a neighborhood that contains some of the world's most valuable real estate. The bulk of the neighborhood lies between Oak Street and Lincoln Park, bounded on the east by Lake Shore Drive, with La Salle Street above Division forming the western margin between the Gold Coast and Old Town.

Until the 1880s, the land here was largely vacant, with some sections, later condemned as "unhealthy," serving as burial grounds. The State Street merchant Potter Palmer broke with the trend of his day, and instead of building his mansion south of the Loop around Prairie Avenue (where so many giants of Chicago industry and commerce had their homes), he went north. In 1882, Palmer built a lakeshore castle bordering marshlands in what was then a relative wilderness. It is said that this prince of Chicago retailing had a speculative scheme in mind when he chose this area for his residence. And indeed the mere presence here of the Potters, then one of the most prominent families in Chicago's high society, served as an instant magnet, drawing the carriage trade to the north in droves. Soon the value of Potter's extensive northside holdings escalated rapidly, as the price of land rose 400% over the course of a few short years. Whether wittingly or by chance, Potter Palmer had spun his marsh grass into gold.

Our itinerary here combines a leisurely stroll on Chicago's downtown strand along Lake Michigan with a walk among the fine town houses that line the tree-shaded interior streets of the Gold Coast.

Take the underpass beneath Michigan Avenue to reach the:

1. **Oak Street Beach.** Enjoy the luxury of a walk in the sand right smack in the middle of downtown Chicago; it may not be Copacabana, but neither New York nor Los Angeles can claim such a bonny downtown amenity. If the sand doesn't suit you, stick to the concrete path, making sure to keep to the pedestrian lane to avoid being run down by a speeding bicyclist. On your right is the sweeping vista of the great inland waterway, Lake Michigan. At some distance, you are almost certain to see signs of the stolid commercial shipping that plies these waters, as one or several vessels crawls along the horizon. While you're ambling along, there's nothing to prevent you from admiring the imposing residential behemoths on the opposite side of Lake Shore Drive. Among the giant structures, take note also of the few remaining mansions, the relics of a gilded age.

    Beginning just above Scott Street, you will see a cluster of four such exemplars of that privileged past, including:

2. **The Carl C. Heissen House,** at 1250 Lake Shore Drive. Also nearby stands the Mason Brayman Starring House, at no. 1254; the Arthur T. Aldis House at no. 1258; and the Lawrence D. Rockwell House at no. 1260. Both the Heissen House (1890) and its immediate neighbor, the Starring House (1889), for example, strongly suggest the longstanding romance of wealthy Chicagoans for the sturdy Romanesque, which soon thereafter gave way to the lighter continental lines of the Second Empire.

    A second cluster of former private mansions, all vaguely

neoclassical in outline and appointments, faces Lake Michigan toward the north end of Oak Street Beach, beginning at:

3. 1516 North Lake Shore Drive. This building is home to the International College of Surgeons, while its neighbor at no. 1525 is a museum belonging to the same institution. The International College of Surgeons Museum houses a fascinating collection of exhibits and artifacts that portray the evolution of medical surgery in what was once a private mansion, designed in 1917 by Chicago architect Howard Van Doren Shaw. Aside from viewing the collection itself, another reason for entering the Surgeons Museum is to view the well-preserved interior of Shaw's creation, including the massive stone staircase and the second-floor library with its fine wood paneling. A third structure, 1530 North Lake Shore Drive, a creation of Benjamin Marshall, is today the Polish Consulate.

This stroll up the beach should take between 15 and 30 minutes. When you reach the end of the sand, continue on the path past the patch of green where the jetty leads out to a harbor light, and into the parking lot. Straight on is the:

4. North Avenue Beach. This is the next strand up the line, on the southern end of Lincoln Park, complete with its own beach house.

Now double back and recross Lake Shore Drive by way of the North Avenue underpass. Continue up North Avenue two blocks to North State Parkway. That imposing residence on your left, surrounded by spacious grounds, is the:

5. residence of the Roman Catholic Archbishop of Chicago. The estate's official address is 1555 North State Parkway. This mansion is an example in red brick of early Queen Anne styling. Archbishop Patrick Feehan was its first resident after the mansion was completed in 1880 on what had been the grounds of a Catholic cemetery that stretched between present-day North Avenue and Schiller Street. By the turn of the century, the Chicago Archdiocese had subdivided much of this remaining Gold Coast property, providing house sites for many affluent families who subsequently moved into the neighborhood. A virtual battalion of chimney pots marches across the roofline of this old episcopal residence, which is one of the oldest and most familiar on the Gold Coast.

Across the street on the opposite corner of North Avenue is:

6. 1550 North State Parkway. Each apartment in this 1912 vintage luxury high rise, known locally as the Benjamin Marshall Building, originally occupied a single floor and contained 15 rooms spread over 9,000 square feet. The architects were Marshall & Fox, highly regarded in their day as builders of fine

THE GOLD COAST

Lincoln Park

North Avenue Beach

Lake Michigan

start here

Oak Street Beach

finish here

1. Oak Street Beach
2. The Carl C. Heisen House
3. 1516 North Lake Shore Drive
4. North Avenue Beach
5. Residence of the Roman Catholic Archbishop of Chicago
6. 1550 North State Parkway
7. Bullock Folsom House
8. 4 West Burton Place
9. Cyrus H. McCormick Mansion
10. 1519 North Astor Street
11. 1451 and 1449 North Astor Street
12. 1443 and 1444 North Astor Street
13. 1427 North Astor Street
14. 1421 North Astor Street
15. 1416 North Astor Street
16. Thomas W. Hinde House
17. Joseph T. Ryerson House
18. Charnley House
19. Astor Court
20. Hefner Hall
21. 1328 North State Parkway
22. James L. Houghteling houses
23. 1301 and 1260 North Astor Street
24. Renaissance Condominiums
25. East Cedar Street
26. Lot P. Smith House
27. Fortnightly of Chicago

6563

hotels. There was once a garden entryway located at the ground-floor level, and among the noteworthy architectural features adorning the exterior of this beaux arts classic are the many small balconies and the bowed windows at the corners of the building.

Continue west for one block on North Avenue and turn left, following Dearborn Street to Burton Place and the:

7. **Bullock Folsom House.** As its telltale mansard roof reveals, this landmark home at 1454 North Dearborn Street is pure Second Empire. That roof, incidentally, is shingled in slate, not asphalt. Neighboring houses at no. 1450 and 1434 have some of the same French influenced ornamentation and styling. Across Burton Place just to the north, at 1500 North Dearborn Street is another example of a rival architectural fashion of the day, the Richardsonian or Romanesque.

Now return to the east again along Burton, but before crossing North State Parkway, stop before:

8. **4 West Burton Place.** Built originally as a private residence in 1902 by Richard E. Schmidt for a family named Madlener, this striking continental structure today houses the Graham Foundation for Advanced Studies in the Fine Arts. There is something very modern about the appearance of this former home; the clean, sleek lines of its ornamentation seem to foreshadow the art deco styling still two decades off.

Now continue on one block further east to Astor Street. On the northwest corner at 1500 North Astor Street is the former:

9. **Cyrus H. McCormick Mansion.** This manse, originally built for the Patterson family in 1893, and designed by New York architect Stanford White, was purchased by Cyrus McCormick, Jr., in 1914. The north addition was added in 1927 by David Adler, doubling the size of the initial building. Like so many of New York's Fifth Avenue mansions, whose design White and his contemporaries had a hand in, the McCormick palazzo is an essay in the neoclassical. Square and grand, like a temple of antiquity, the construction combines Roman bricks of burnt yellow with touches of terra-cotta for the trim.

The tour loops north briefly on Astor Street to take in a home of historical interest:

10. **1519 North Astor Street.** This attractive town house was once the residence of Robert Todd Lincoln, the only surviving child of Abraham and Mary Todd Lincoln. The younger Lincoln took up the private practice of law in Chicago after the Civil War. He remained in Chicago for much of the remainder of his life, leaving on two occasions during the 1880s and '90s to serve in the administrations of several Presidents, first under James Garfield and Chester A. Arthur as Secretary of War, and later

under Benjamin Harrison as minister to Britain. On the death of George Pullman, one of his major corporate clients, Lincoln assumed the presidency of the Pullman Palace Car Company in 1897.

Reversing direction again, walking south along Astor Street, notice two houses at:

11. **1451 and 1449 North Astor Street.** The former, occupying the corner lot, is the work of Howard Van Doren Shaw, built in 1910 according to the so-called "Jacobethan" fashion. This somewhat obscure term combines the words Jacobean and Elizabethan, and described a revival form of certain 16th- and 17th-century features of English architecture, including narrow, elongated windows, split-level roofs, and multiple chimney stacks. The house at no. 1449 was built around the turn of the century, but the architect of this glorious château remains a mystery. Guarding the home's entrance is a somewhat intimidating stone porch, seemingly out of scale. Among the home's other unique characteristics are the big front bay and the frieze below the cornice, a scroll of stylized shells.

Two other neighboring homes of interest, facing each other across the street are:

12. **1443 and 1444 North Astor Street.** According to one Chicago author, the May House at no. 1443 "bears a resemblance to H. H. Richardson's Glessner House," the historic landmark located south of the Loop at 1800 South Prairie Avenue. Facing this home directly across Astor Street is no. 1444, a true sampler of the Chicago art deco style, built in 1929 by Holabird and Roche. Next walk to:

13. **1427 North Astor Street.** The dean of Chicago architects and pioneer of the earliest skyscrapers, William Le Baron Jenny designed this structure in 1889. Today this home is on the market for an asking price of $3 million! Many of the neighboring homes are valued in this range (give or take a million). This will give you some idea of why they call this neighborhood the Gold Coast.

Several doors down is:

14. **1421 North Astor Street.** This somewhat fanciful but very appealing cottage was once the base in Chicago of a Catholic missionary order, the Maryknoll Fathers.

Across the street is:

15. **1416 North Astor Street.** This was another Gold Coast residence belonging to the McCormick clan.

The neighboring structure at 1412 North Astor Street is the:

16. **Thomas W. Hinde House.** This 1892 home, created by Douglas S. Pentecost, is a study in Flemish architecture of the late Middle Age. The facade has been altered, but some of the

---

THE McCORMICKS OF CHICAGO

Cyrus Jr. was the son of Cyrus H. McCormick, the man credited with the invention of the reaper, perhaps the single most important mechanical advancement of its day in agriculture. The reaper made it possible to farm huge tracts of wheat on the fertile prairie without depending on seasonal labor for its harvest. The senior McCormick, a native of Virginia, had built his first factory in Chicago in 1847. Wiped out by the fire of 1871, the McCormicks were able to rebuild easily, since the demand for the company's farm implements was by then firmly established, and the family fortune already made several times over.

So many members of the McCormick family once occupied homes near Rush and Erie streets just south of the Gold Coast, that their neighborhood became known as "McCormicksville." Cyrus Jr. became the first president of International Harvester when the McCormick Harvesting Company merged with several of its former competitors in 1902. The McCormicks were no friends of the working class; their plant was an ongoing target of labor agitation during the 1880s. A rally at the McCormick plant in 1886, during which a worker was killed by the police, fueled the infamous Haymarket Affair on the following night.

---

original stone ornamentation remains, as do such dominant features as the multipaned diamond-shaped windows.

On the same side of the street at 1406 North Astor Street is the:

17. **Joseph T. Ryerson House.** David Adler designed this 1922 landmark home in the manner of a Parisian hotel, like those buildings of scale and delicacy that even to this day line such Left Bank streets as rue St-Jacques. Adler himself supervised the 1931 addition of the top floor and the mansard roof. Woven into the wrought-iron grillwork above the entrance are the initials of the original owner.

The next house to warrant our attention is also a landmark, one that incarnates the collaborative genius of three giants of American architecture. At 1365 North Astor Street, on the southeast corner of Schiller Street stands the:

18. **Charnley House.** A then-obscure draftsman, Frank Lloyd Wright, played a major role in designing this 1892 home, shortly before he left the firm of Adler and Sullivan to launch his own

storied career. The house seems suitable to our modern world though it's located in this fairyland neighborhood where most residences have borrowed their shapes and forms from antiquity or the medieval past. This is either because Wright was so perceptively and organically in tune with the special needs of the American domestic landscape, or because there is actually something timeless, even universal, in his ideas that transcends his time and culture and carries over from one region to another, from one generation to the next.

Continuing down the block, pause before 1355 North Astor Street, known as:

19. Astor Court. Row houses are not common in spacious, once land-rich Chicago, so this multiple unit is rare on that account. But it's also noteworthy as a window on the Georgian formality that is much more characteristic of parts of London. Because of the ornament above the central entrance, the building is sometimes referred to by its nickname, "the court of the golden hands." To the right is the original drive, a formal inner court is surrounded by additional residential units.

Return now to Schiller Street and walk west to State Parkway. Cross the street and turn left, continuing south along State until roughly the middle of the block where you'll come to:

20. Hefner Hall. This bulky mansion at 1340 North State Parkway was built in 1899 for an upright Calvinist named George S. Isham. And despite the fact that Playboy's Hugh Hefner lived here during the heyday of his Chicago years, the place still has the whiff of the countinghouse about it. Here old Hugh romped with his pretty bunnies, the commodities around which his own fortune was made, and perfected the airbrushed version of erotica and cracker barrel hedonism that once made him the nation's reigning purveyor of softcore porn.

A renowned contemporary architect had his hand in our next stop:

21. 1328 North State Parkway. Bertrand Goldberg, of Marina City fame—the pine cone–like mixed residential, commercial, nautical towers across from the Loop on the Chicago River— remodeled what were originally two separate homes on this property. The two 1938 vintage dwellings were connected in 1956 to serve as studio and home for Goldberg's mother-in-law, sculptor Lillian Florsheim.

REFUELING STOP At the corner of State Parkway and Goethe Street, on the ground floor of the Omni Ambassador East Hotel, is the celebrated **Pump Room** (tel. 266-0630), traditionally Chicago's premier watering hole. Any celebrity passing through Chicago worked the local gossip columnists from Booth One. Today, the Pump Room remains a fine and somewhat pricey restaurant; it's also a great place to have a cocktail and indulge in a bit of people-watching.

Our tour swings one block east again, back to Astor Street by way of Goethe Street. Turn left and at 1308–1312 North Astor Street look at the:

22. **James L. Houghteling houses.** Here's an eclectic cluster of Chicago town houses built by Burnham and Root between 1887 and 1888. Originally there were four dwellings, but no. 1306 was torn down. John Wellborn Root, who is credited with the design of the buildings, actually lived here with his family in no. 1310. Here the brilliant architect also met his untimely end at the age of 40.

On opposite corners diagonally across Goethe Street are two apartment towers which represent the trend toward high-rise living within the interior streets of the Gold Coast, beginning in the 1930s:

23. **1301 and 1260 North Astor Street.** Constructed by Philip B. Maher in 1932 and 1931 respectively, these two apartment buildings are classics of the sleek modernism that characterized American commercial architecture after World War I. 1300 North Astor Street, on the other hand, is a 1960s version of the high-rise apartment house, by Bertrand Goldberg, of a form that seemed so avant garde in that period (like the fins on Detroit gas guzzlers) and which today seems dated.

Now we get a chance to stretch our legs a bit on this quiet lane-like-street that seems so protected behind the wall of towering condominiums on Lake Shore Drive. Walk two blocks south on Astor Street to the corner of Division Street. The old building on the right is the:

24. **Renaissance Condominiums.** The address is 1200 North Astor Street, and the building was the design of Holabird and Roche, dating from 1897. This is one of the rare examples of a Chicago school building on the north side. Notice its similarity in construction to the buildings of the same vintage that remain in the Loop, especially the brick work and the window bays.

Turn right on Division Street and walk one block west to Rush Street. Turn left, staying on the east side of Rush, and proceed two blocks south to:

25. **East Cedar Street.** It's worth taking a stroll down this long block between Rush Street and Lake Shore Drive, because much of the turn-of-the-century scale of things has been so well preserved. Some of the homes of later vintage are also unique

and elegant. See in particular the two clusters of "cottages" nos. 42–48 (1896), and 50–54 (1892). These homes provide added evidence of the once widespread popularity in Chicago of the Romanesque styling in domestic architecture. The first group was built by State Street merchant prince, Potter Palmer.

Return now to Rush Street and walk to the next block south, turn left on Bellevue Place where, among the homes of interest, you will see 32 East Bellevue Place, the:

26. Lot P. Smith House. It took a certain kind of head, even in 1887 when this delightful place was built, to name your child "Lot." In any event, this Lot had both the righteous good fortune and the good sense to have had his home designed by John Wellborn Root.

At the end of the block, not far from Lake Shore Drive, is our final stop in the Gold Coast, 120 East Bellevue Place, the:

27. Fortnightly of Chicago. Built by the New York architect Charles F. McKim—a partner of Stanford White—while sojourning in Chicago as a lead designer of the World's Columbian Exposition, the design of this mansion helped to herald in the Georgian fashion in architecture that would replace the earlier preference for Romanesque Revival throughout the Gold Coast. A woman's literary club has occupied the premises since 1922.

REFUELING STOP Another fine and venerable Chicago hotel, the **Drake** (tel. 787-2200), offers the perfect haven for some post-walking tour refreshment, for cocktails in the swank surroundings of the Palm Court or ice cream and tea in the Oak Terrace. Just continue down Bellevue Place to Lake Shore Drive and cross to the hotel entrance two short blocks south at Walton Street.

Lincoln Park

Start: The grounds of the Chicago Historical Society, Clark Street at North Avenue, at the southern end of Lincoln Park.
Public Transportation: CTA bus nos. 11, 22, 36, 72, 151, and 156 stop nearby.
Finish: The Chicago Historical Society.
Time: 1½ hours for the walk; add 2 additional hours if you decide to really explore the zoo and the two museums featured on this itinerary.
Best Times: When the zoo and museums are open. Schedules are listed below for the museums; the zoo is open daily from 8am to 5:15pm (its buildings are open from 9am to 5pm.
Worst Times: When the zoo and museums are closed.

Lincoln Park is the largest and most popular park in Chicago. Long and narrow, the park accompanies Lake Michigan's shoreline for almost six miles, and comprises an area of over 1,200 acres. In the summertime, Lincoln Park is virtually spilling over with the crowds who gather there to take their leisure in a variety of ways, especially on the weekends, and most heavily at the various lakefront beaches. Since the park, and one of its principal attractions, the zoo, is open year round, a visit there is never really out of season.

The itinerary of this walking tour is grouped into five main elements: the park, the zoo, a stroll down Lincoln Park West, and visits to two museums, the Academy of Sciences and the Chicago Historical Society. In reality, our walk through the park will concern itself primarily with a detailed exploration of the attractive Lincoln Park Zoo, but will highlight a handful of other park attractions that fall within the area we'll be visiting between North and Belden avenues.

Our tour begins on the grounds behind the Historical Society at the:

1. **Statue of Abraham Lincoln.** This impressive monument, also known as "The Standing Lincoln," was completed in 1887 by the Dublin-born sculptor Augustus Saint-Gaudens. Saint-Gaudens, the son of an Irish mother and French father, was brought to New York City as an infant, and apprenticed at age 13 to a cameo cutter. He would later become the most celebrated American sculptor of the late 19th century. The subject of Lincoln was dear to Saint-Gaudens, who executed two major likenesses of the fallen president, based to some degree on his personal observations, once when the president was still living, and then, following the assassination, when Lincoln's remains lay in state. This work, which shows Lincoln poised to begin a public address, also benefits from the life casts of Lincoln's face and hands executed by the sculptor Leonard Volk.

   Now, enter the park proper by way of a subterranean walk under La Salle and follow the formal, tree-lined path bordering the lagoon to the entrance of the:

2. **Farm in the Zoo.** There is no admittance charge; the Lincoln Park Zoo, open every day of the year, is among the last free zoological parks in the world. This replica of a farm on the prairie was completed in the 1960s. Featured on the five-acre plot are a working dairy barn, a horse barn, a livestock shed, a poultry coop, a produce garden, and a large barn-like educational facility where regularly scheduled programs are geared toward helping urban residents understand the importance of agriculture and the American farmer. This is very much a hands-on facility, and is particularly popular with school-age children. The Farm in the Zoo's cows, incidentally, yield about 20 gallons of fresh milk daily, and the 30 or so chickens lay an average of two dozen eggs a week.

   When you exit the farm, continue on the path along the:

3. **South Lagoon.** South Lagoon is a perennial favorite among Chicagoans for row boating and paddle boating and, at least in winters past, provided an outdoor pond for ice skating as well. The lagoon has recently undergone a well justified and major rehabilitation, for it was here that the zoo had its modest beginnings in 1868, when the park received a pair of trumpeter

swans as a gift from the Central Park Zoo in New York City. The swan, whose image may be seen throughout the park, remains the symbol of the Lincoln Park Zoo.

The imposing building to your immediate left as you walk along the lagoon path, is a national landmark, listed on the National Register of Historical Places, the:

4. Café Brauer. This stunning Prairie-style café was built in 1908 to replace a large Victorian boathouse that once occupied the same spot along the edge of the lagoon. Café Brauer, operated as a continental-style restaurant between 1912 and 1941, was restored in 1990 at a cost of $4.2 million, and is again open for business today, housing a cafeteria called Zoo Food, the Ice Cream Shoppe, and a large banquet hall available for private parties.

Just beyond Café Brauer is an entrance to the zoo. Notice the many formal plantings and flower gardens, which, incidentally, are tended and maintained by a small army of over 1,000 docents and volunteer gardeners.

Our tour will be abbreviated, highlighting some of the zoo's most popular attractions. For our first exhibit, follow signs toward the:

5. Antelope and Zebra Area. This is an outdoor habitat for a variety of hoof stock from around the world, including American bison, reindeer, zebras, the Arabian oryx, and the Bactrian camel. This zoo played an important historical role in the preservation of the American bison, which was virtually exterminated by the end of the 19th century.

ZOO FACTS

- Biggest animal: Binti, an African elephant weighing over three tons.
- Smallest animal: The poison dart frog, the size of a dime.
- Total number of lowland gorillas born at the zoo: 31.
- Number of endangered species at the zoo: 44.
- A typical weekly food order: 750 lbs. of carrots; 2,034 apples; 1,575 bananas; 100 lbs. of onions; 450 lbs. of lettuce; 460 lbs. of sweet potatoes; 9,000 crickets; 12,000 meal worms; 785 rats and mice; 405 lbs. of feline and canine meat; 50 lbs. of horse meat; 850 lbs. of herring; and four boxes of eucalyptus (flown in from Florida twice weekly for the koalas). And that's only a partial list!
- The zoo's annual grocery bill: $350,000.

LINCOLN PARK

W. Fullerton Pkwy.

N. Clark St.

W. Webster Ave.

N. Lincoln Park West

Stockton Dr.

N. Sedgwick St.

Armitage

N. Lincoln Ave.

W. Wisconsin St.

N. Clark St.

W. Menomonee St.

W. Eugenie St.

N. Wells St.

N. LaSalle St.

North Ave.

Lake Shore Dr.

Cannon Dr.

Simonds Dr.

Ridge Dr.

Zoo

South Pond

Lincoln

Park

Lake

Michigan

41

start here

La Salle Dr.

finish here

North Blvd.

0 440 y
   402 m

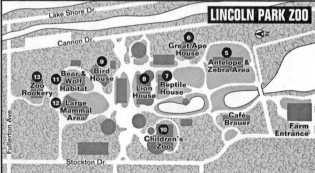

LINCOLN PARK ZOO

Lake Shore Dr.

Cannon Dr.

Fullerton Ave.

Zoo Rookery

Bear & Wolf Habitat

Bird House

Large Mammal Area

Great Ape House

Antelope & Zebra Area

Lion House

Reptile House

Café Brauer

Farm Entrance

Children's Zoo

Stockton Dr.

1 Statue of Abraham Lincoln
2 Farm in the Zoo
3 South Lagoon
4 Café Brauer
5 Antelope and Zebra Area
6 Lester E. Fisher Great Ape House
7 Reptile House
8 Kovler Lion House
9 McCormick Bird House and Regenstein Bird of Prey Exhibit
10 Pritzker Children's Zoo
11 Robert R. McCormick Bear and Wolf Habitat
12 Joseph Regenstein Large Mammal Area
13 Zoo Rookery
14 Lincoln Park Conservatory
15 Bust of Sir Georg Solti
16 Bates Fountain
17 William Shakespeare statue
18 Belden-Stratford Apartments
19 2236–2258 North Lincoln Park West
20 Chicago Academy of Sciences
21 Grave of David Kennison
22 Couch Mausoleum
23 Chicago Historical Society

Next stop is the nearby:

6. Lester E. Fisher Great Ape House. Named for a man who served as director of Lincoln Park for 30 years, the Great Ape House was opened in 1976, and is today home to the largest captive lowland gorilla collection in the United States. The area houses six modern habitats for family groups of gorillas, chimpanzees, and orangutans. One ape named Sinbad can no longer run free with the troops; he's been confined to his cage because of "antisocial" behavior.

A few more steps along the pathway brings you to the:

7. Reptile House. Snakes do exercise a fascination—from a distance and behind a thick sheet of plate glass. The zoo has an extensive collection of the slippery, slithery creatures in all sizes, shapes, and colors. And the Reptile House has gained a national reputation among the experts as a kind of successful old folks' home for snakes. The Society for the Study of Reptiles and Amphibians has recognized the facility for housing seven species holding longevity records in the United States.

Behind the Reptile House is:

8. Kovler Lion House. This combination denning enclosure and naturalistic outdoor habitat is home to the zoo's world-class collection of endangered and threatened big cats. Tiger aficionados will especially like this exhibit; there are huge slinky Siberians, and the Bengals can be seen lounging about in their front yard, separated from their potential human prey by a wide, deep moat.

Next on our list is the:

9. McCormick Bird House and Regenstein Birds of Prey Exhibit. Originally opened in 1904, the Bird House was recently reopened after a $2.8 million renovation. The renovated update contains 10 new and improved habitats re-creating six different ecosystems with lush landscaping. Take your chances in the free-flight area; once an exotic bird landed on my shoulder, which I took as a good omen. (Of course, there's always a possibility that something else might land on your shoulder.)

There's a catch-22 provision associated with the Birds of Prey Exhibit. Some species can't be kept in captivity unless there's something wrong with them. The bald eagles on display, for example, are among the walking wounded; one is lame, the other blind. Also in residence here are the usual gang of road-kill scavengers, owls, vultures, and a host of other well-loved raptors.

Seeing the next exhibit requires a brief reversal of direction. When leaving the McCormick Bird House, look for signs indicating the location of the:

10. Pritzker Children's Zoo. When it opened in 1959, this was the first indoor children's zoo in the country. The central

BUSHMAN AND PERKINS: NATIONAL CELEBRITIES AT THE LINCOLN PARK ZOO

On August 15, 1930, a 38-pound, 2½-year-old gorilla from French Cameroon arrived at the Lincoln Park Zoo, and was at the time one of only five gorillas in captivity. At full maturity, Bushman weighed in at 550 pounds. By the time he died in 1951, Bushman had achieved a celebrity status way beyond the confines of Chicago. Notre Dame coach Knute Rockne, hearing that Bushman liked to play football, sent the gorilla an autographed ball. Members of the Alexander Dumas Gourmand Club in France made Bushman an honorary member when they learned that he had devoured 22 pounds of food at one sitting. Bushman appeared countless times in newsreels, and on the pages of such national magazines as *Look* and *Life*. When Bushman died, thousands filed past his empty cage to pay their last respects, and the interior of the Monkey House was renamed Bushman Hall in his honor. His cage remains empty, and is open to the public; you can actually go in and sit on the old fellow's former chair.

Marlin Perkins was a primate, too, who most of the time lived outside the cages where the other zoo residents were housed. Perkins, in fact, was a director of the zoo who rose to national prominence on "Zoo Parade," an NBC-TV network nature show that ran from 1949 to 1957, and was broadcast weekly from the Lincoln Park Zoo. Perkins then moved on to the equally popular "Wild Kingdom," which also aired for many years. Perkins's very public leadership role is credited with having made Lincoln Park Zoo the most heavily attended zoo in the world during the 1950s—as it is today—with an annual attendance of over four million visitors.

attraction here is a display of North American wildlife in an exotic garden setting. During the warm weather months, there are educational, live animal presentations in the outdoor amphitheater. The zoo's nursery is also located here, as is a petting zoo, featuring African pygmy goats. Another popular educational program, called "Conversation Corner," is a hands-on learning center for children.

THE GUAM RAILS

The McCormick Bird House contains a variety of endangered species, like the Guam Rails, only a few score of which are known to be extant in the world today. And only a handful of them are at the Lincoln Park Zoo. A pair of these mature adults were recently joined by a nest of chicks—four in all—following a delicate and painstaking rebreeding program. The successful hatchings occurred after the ground-nesting birds were moved from a 194-square-foot home to a 506-square-foot indoor naturalistic habitat. Almost all the eggs that had been laid in the smaller habitat were broken. As part of the Guam Rail Species Survival Plan, some of the chicks hatched at the Lincoln Park Zoo will be reintroduced into the wild, on the island of Rota, 31 miles north of Guam, where the birds originate. Guam Rails are extinct in the wild, with those in captivity numbering about 150, down drastically from an estimated wild population of 80,000 in 1968.

Now return to the eastern side of the zoo, and continue on to the:

11. **Robert R. McCormick Bear and Wolf Habitat.** The main attraction here is a 266,000-gallon polar bear pool with an underwater viewing window. The wolf, too, is an endless source of fascination, our domestic Fido's evolutionary predecessor, and a species of "dog" who was never brought to heel.

Just beyond the Bear and Wolf Habitat is the:

12. **Joseph Regenstein Large Mammal Area.** This uniquely designed building features indoor and outdoor habitats for a wide variety of medium- to large-sized mammals. There are capybaras and tapirs from the Amazon; timberwolves from the snowy north; giraffes, rhinos, and hippos from central Africa; and several elephants, including a very special one named Shanti. On November 11, 1990, a 15-year-old African elephant named Bozie gave birth to Shanti, the first elephant ever born in the state of Illinois. Shanti, whose birth can be witnessed within the pavilion on video, first hit the scales at a whopping 270 pounds.

Here our tour of the zoo comes to an end. Exit by way of the Conservatory entrance. But before leaving, check to see if one more very special park environment is again open to the public, the:

13. **Zoo Rookery.** This natural environment for birds has been called "one of the city's most evocative landscapes." The

LINCOLN PARK • 89

landscaping was inspired by Japanese formalism, but its content, both geologic and vegetable, is purely midwestern. The level of seclusion offered by the Rookery, however, creates a security problem; until this is worked out, the Rookery will remain closed.

On the way out of the park there are several other points of interest, including the:

14. Lincoln Park Conservatory. Inside are four great halls filled with thousands of plants, the closest thing that Chicago has to a botanical garden within the city limits. The Palm House is resplendent with giant palms and rubber trees, while the Fernery nurtures plants that grow close to the forest floor and the Tropical House is a symphony of shiny greenery. The fourth hall, Show House, showcases seasonal floral exhibitions. The conservatory is open daily from 9am to 5pm; admission is free.

A few paces south of the conservatory entrance is a large, modern sculpture, a:

15. bust of Sir Georg Solti. Until his retirement in the early 1990s, Solti was so highly regarded as the musical director of the Chicago Symphony that he rated a public statue while still living.

Beyond the homage to Solti is a French formal garden, a beautiful sight to behold from late spring through October. In the midst of that garden is the:

16. Bates Fountain. Also known as "Storks at Play," the fountain is the combined work of Augustus Saint-Gaudens and his former pupil, Frederick William MacMonnies.

Leave the park along the path that runs in front of the conservatory; on your way to the street, you'll pass through an English garden, that is to say a well-pruned wood lot, selectively planted with a variety of trees and shrubs. Just before emerging onto Lincoln Park West at Belden Avenue, behold the statue of the seated:

17. William Shakespeare. This is one of many public statues in the park whose upkeep has corporate sponsorship thanks to the "Adopt a Monument" program promoted by a group called Friends of Lincoln Park. Among the other park statues under their care are those of LaSalle, Schiller, Franklin, Grant, Goethe, and Hans Christian Andersen.

Across the street is an apartment building, 2300 North Lincoln Park West, that once functioned as a swank northside hotel, the:

18. Belden-Stratford Apartments. From the point of view of a culinary sophisticate, the most interesting thing about this building today is that it is home to two fine restaurants, Le Grand Café, and the super-chic Ambria, which in a 1993 *Travel and Leisure* readership survey was listed as number 25 among the 100 best restaurants in the country. Whether or not you choose to eat at either of these worthy establishments while in Chicago, take a moment now to enter the Belden-Stratford to see the lobby, and, if possible, to peek inside the Ambria dining room, a paradigm of continental-style elegance.

Now take a leisurely stroll down Lincoln Park West. There are two sites to point out along this route, less for their intrinsic value than for their vicarious link to Chicago's two most revered architects:

19. 2236–2258 North Lincoln Park West. This block of homes was designed by Simeon B. Eisendrath, an apprentice in the firm of Louis H. Sullivan. Further down the avenue, where Lincoln Park West terminates at Clark Street, a set of row houses at 2103–2117 North Clark Street and 310–312 West Dickens Avenue was designed by Joseph Lyman Silsbee, the architect Frank Lloyd Wright first worked for when he arrived in Chicago.

REFUELING STOP Also on the corner at Dickens Avenue is **R. J. Crunts,** 2056 Lincoln Park West. This is a very popular neighborhood restaurant with an extensive menu of chicken dishes, burgers, pasta plates, and the like. There's also a first-rate salad bar, and a knock-out Sunday brunch that's all you can eat, but is sometimes too crowded to accommodate all comers.

As we near the end of the tour, there are still two very important Chicago institutions to visit, so try to allow sufficient time to explore these very informative collections, first at the:

20. Chicago Academy of Sciences. The Academy has housed its natural history collection at this location, 2001 North Clark Street (tel. 549-0606), since 1893, the year this attractive, four-story Renaissance Revival building was inaugurated. Originally, however, the Academy—which dates from 1857, making it Chicago's oldest museum—occupied two prior locations, both in the Loop, and both destroyed by fire. Eclipsed somewhat in importance as an institution dedicated to science on a broad scale by the creation of the Field Museum in Grant Park, the Academy narrowed its focus and concentrated more on local natural history. Its well-known dioramas of Midwest habitats began to be developed in 1915. These dioramas depict communities in the Chicago area as they existed a hundred years ago or more. The Academy's snake collection is considered the most extensive in the entire world.

Today this small museum serves the Chicago community as an extension of the classroom. It is doubtful that a single child goes through the Chicago school system without making at least one field trip to the Chicago Academy of Sciences. The institution is ideally suited for this role. The nature displays are well presented, and a lot is packed into a relatively small area. One is not overwhelmed here by the enormity of the collection, which can be viewed satisfactorily in a short space of time. A half hour here—unlike in most museums—can be time well spent. Open daily, except Christmas Day, from 10am to 5pm. There is a small admission charge.

There's a narrow strip of parkland running along Clark Street near the Farm in the Zoo. Here you will find a most unusual sight on a large boulder marked with a plaque, the:

21. grave of David Kennison. Most of what is today the southern end of Lincoln Park was once Chicago's municipal

ROBERT KENNICOTT, FOUNDER OF THE ACADEMY OF SCIENCES

This obscure naturalist, who died at the age of 31 on a remote beach during an expedition in the Yukon, was one of the most promising young scientists of his day. He was only 22 when he helped to found the Academy of Sciences, which was based substantially on specimens Kennicott had already collected during his youth, and while conducting a survey of natural resources on the land belonging to the Illinois Central Railroad. Kennicott was also the Academy's first curator. Later, Kennicott's explorations would take him to regions of the Arctic in Alaska and Canada where he was among the first white men to be seen. At the time of his death, Kennicott had not only assembled what is often referred to as the most extensive collection of plant and animal specimens of the 19th century, but he had also compiled eyewitness reports from Alaska that reportedly helped convince the U.S. government to purchase that vast territory from the Russians. While on an expedition in 1866 to help survey a telegraph route to Europe across the Bering Strait and by way of Siberia, Kennicott rescued a Russian whose boat had begun to sink from the freezing water. The man had stolen the boat and was attempting to abandon the expedition. The next morning Kennicott's body was found on a beach of the Yukon River, his death the apparent result of a heart attack. Before dying, he had scratched a map of the surrounding region in the sand.

cemetery, running from North to Webster avenues. Reinterment of the many remains within burial grounds outside the city limits was not completed until 1874, almost a decade after the park was opened. Somehow, the grave of this historic figure was left undisturbed. Kennison was truly one of a kind. He was born in 1736, and died 115 years later in 1852. His lifetime spanned the French and Indian War, the Revolutionary War, and the Boston Tea Party, of which, according to legend, he was the oldest surviving participant.

Crossing La Salle Street, and continuing on Clark Street enroute to our final stop, you will pass the:

22. **Couch Mausoleum.** This is the only family tomb that remains from the old cemetery. The Couch family went all the way to the Illinois Supreme Court in their efforts to block its removal. In a final macabre note about the old municipal cemetery, now and then when the city digs here for one purpose or another, a few spare bones are uncovered from a grave that the interment team unwittingly overlooked.

We have now come full circle, and our final treat is a visit to one of Chicago's most interesting and unique museums, the:

23. **Chicago Historical Society,** Clark Street at North Avenue (tel. 642-4600). "People make history. But it's the objects they leave behind . . . that allow us to interpret the past." That line from the Historical Society brochure sums up with elegant simplicity the enduring appeal of this institution's collection. Those "objects" as displayed in the Chicago Historical Society, especially the American Wing, are as compelling and evocative as any I have ever seen. History buffs will find it hard to tear themselves away from two exhibits in particular, "We the People" and "A House Divided." The gift shop here is also worthy of mention for its many titles of books treating various themes of Chicago's own past.

The collection merits an extended visit, but for those taking this tour whose time is limited, or who have simply run out of gas absorbing the other sights along the way, the following abbreviated inventory of "not to be missed items" can be viewed in just a half hour:

- Benjamin West's 1771 painting, *Penn's Treaty with the Indians*
- Paul Revere's engraving of the 1770 Boston Massacre
- Amos Doolittle's four engravings of the battles of Lexington and Concord
- One of 23 surviving copies of the broadside of the Declaration of Independence printed in Philadelphia on the evening of July 4th, 1776

- A powder horn engraved by a Revolutionary War soldier with such symbols as the Tree of Liberty
- An original watercolor sketch of the first rendering of the U.S. flag authorized by the Continental Congress in 1777
- The U.S. Constitution as first printed in a Philadelphia newspaper, along with an original version of the Bill of Rights with 17 amendments
- *The Railsplitter*, an unknown artist's painting of Lincoln displayed at Republican Party rallies during the 1860 election
- Slave shackles and slave tags
- A first printing of *Uncle Tom's Cabin*
- John Brown's Bible
- The table on which Lincoln drafted the Emancipation Proclamation, and a commemorative copy of the 13th Amendment abolishing slavery, signed by Lincoln, among other government officials
- Lincoln's last dispatch to Grant, and the table on which Lee signed the surrender at Appomattox
- Lincoln's deathbed, and Alonzo Chappel's 1868 painting, *The Death of Lincoln*

REFUELING STOP The **Big Shoulders Café**, located in a corner wing of the Chicago Historical Society, offers one of the most interesting light meal menus in the city. The London broil salad is delicious, as is the jalapeño cornbread served with each meal.

The Chicago Historical Society is open Monday to Saturday from 9:30am to 4:30pm, Sunday from noon to 5pm. There is an admission charge.

WALKING TOUR 8

Old Town

Start: The southwest corner of Clark Street and North Avenue, across from the Chicago Historical Society.

Public Transportation: There are several El stops on the fringes of Old Town, all of which would require some walking to get to this tour's starting point. On the Howard line, the nearest stops are at Clark/Division and North/Clybourn; on the Ravenswood line, the nearest stop is at North and Sedgwick. Your best bet is the bus; nos. 11, 22, 36, 52, 151, and 156 all stop at or near the Chicago Historical Society.

Finish: 1211 North La Salle Street (just across from the Clark/Division stop of the Howard line train.).

Time: 2 hours.

Best Times: Daylight hours; best on the weekends, especially Saturday when street life is most intense. There are stretches along this walk where a reasonable vigilance should be exercised. Old Town has become increasingly fashionable since the 1960s, but pockets of poverty remain, and the relative proximity of Cabrini Green, one of the most disastrous experiments ever in low-income housing, makes it necessary to issue this word of caution.

Worst Times: After dark; unless, of course, the purpose of your visit is to sample Old Town's nightlife, and not to walk through this itinerary.

When you consider that Chicago itself was not officially founded until 1833, the rapid settlement of this area throughout the 1840s lends historical justification to its designation as "Old Town." The early arrivals were primarily Germans who in that decade had begun to flee the continent in great numbers due to crop failures, famine, and the decline of cottage industry. On this land just to the north of more "urban" districts in what is today the Loop, the Near West Side, and River North, the immigrants found the earth suitable for truck farming, and cultivated essentially crops that were staples in their own daily diet: potatoes, cabbage, and celery.

By 1852, German Catholics were plentiful enough to found the parish of St. Michael's, which by the end of the century was the largest German congregation in the city. The farms gradually disappeared as Chicago spread northward and Old Town became absorbed within the encroaching urban hustle and bustle. But North Avenue, with its many specialty shops and beer halls, retained its ethnic flavor, and for years was known as German Broadway. The arrival of substantial industry, like the Oscar Mayer Sausage Company, plus a brewery and piano factory, provided Old Town with a level of economic self-sufficiency. Many residents were able to duplicate a town life similar to the one they had left behind, living and working in the same community.

The 1871 Chicago Fire swept through Old Town and destroyed much of the neighborhood. The walls of St. Michael's withstood the inferno, as did a handful of homes, which are today treasured relics of an early stage of Chicago's life otherwise virtually consumed by the blaze. First shanties, then more permanent wooden cottages, went up in the reconstruction years immediately following the Great Fire. By 1874, rigorous building codes governed the types of structures that Chicagoans could build thereafter, but much of this interim housing was allowed to stand, and some of it survives to this day. Old Town retained its German flavor well into the 1930s, and even now the many shells of the Germans' clubs and institutions remain as testament to the heyday of that culture.

Gradually the ethnic complexion of Old Town began to change, as a wider spectrum of groups took up residence here and the Germans climbed a rung or two on the socio-economic ladder and moved further north. By World War II, the neighborhood was in decline, and the stage was set for its discovery by an advance guard of bohemians and artists. The 1960s saw parts of Old Town—especially the Wells Street area—transformed into the Chicago equivalent of Haight Ashbury and the East Village. In due time, the psychedelic revolution ran its course; the head shops disappeared, but many of the "alternative" theatrical and comedy clubs stayed and prospered. Eventually, the remaining larger businesses—including in recent years the Oscar Mayer plant and Dr. Scholl's factory—closed their doors. With the almost complete gentrification of Lincoln Park to the north and east, Old Town soon took its place as a prime real estate market for people of means who chose to remain near their jobs in downtown Chicago rather than commute to town from the suburbs. At present, Old Town combines these two roles: bedroom community for middle- to upper-income Chicagoans, and entertainment zone for the entire city, featuring some of the best known and most respected comedy clubs in the country.

Our tour begins by taking in a few institutional sites along this stretch of Clark Street. First, at 1536 North Clark Street, is the:

1. **Germania Club.** Among the German-Americans, singing societies provided a significant outlet for social encounters in their community. The "sangverein" originally housed in this elaborately ornamented terra-cotta structure came together around the circumstances of a national tragedy. The club began in 1865 when 300 German-American Civil War veterans formed a men's choir to sing at the funeral of Abraham Lincoln. But only with the construction of this hall in 1889 did the Germania Club achieve a permanent home. Today, a bank is housed in a section of the building, but you can see some of the club's fine original stained-glass windows by entering the lobby.

   Across the street, with its entrance facing North Avenue, is a building of no particular architectural interest, but which houses the prestigious Latin School of Chicago, founded in 1888. Cross North Avenue and walk on the west side of Clark Street in a northerly direction. Directly across from the Chicago Historical Society is the:

2. **Moody Memorial Church.** Dwight L. Moody was one of a handful of colorful American evangelists who made his mark internationally by preaching the "old time religion" of revivalism. Moody came to Chicago from Massachusetts in 1856, and prospered as a shoe salesman. He soon turned away from business to undertake missionary work in the city's poorer sections, working initially under the auspices of the YMCA. Moody's original church, where the Moody Bible Institute is now located at Chicago Avenue and La Salle Street, rapidly became one of the largest congregations in the city. This church on Clark Street was not built until 1925, a quarter century after Moody's death. Echoes of the Byzantine and Romanesque can be seen in the building's design, especially the strong influence of Istanbul's Hagia Sophia.

   Walk to the corner and cross La Salle Street, turning left onto Eugenie Street. Nos. 215, 217, 219, and 225 are pre-1874:

OLD TOWN

880 y
805 m

Lincoln Park

Webster Ave.
Dickens Ave.
W. Armitage Ave.
W. Wisconsin St.
W. Menomonee St.
W. Willow St.
W. Eugenie St.
W. North Ave.
W. Blackhawk St.
Burton Pl.
W. Schiller St.
Evergreen Ave.
Goethe St.
W. Scott St.
W. Division St.
W. Elm St.
Hill St.
Wendell St.
Oak St.
Locust St.

N. Fremont
N. Dayton St.
N. Halsted St.
N. Burling St.
Orchard St.
N. Howe St.
N. Larrabee St.
N. Mohawk St.
N. Cleveland Ave.
N. Sedgwick St.
Lincoln Ave.
N. Clark St.
N. Park Ave.
N. Wells St.
N. La Salle St.
N. Bissell St.
N. Clybourn Ave.
Ogden Ave.
N. Crosby St.
N. Kingsbury St.
Hooker St.
N. Branch St.
Chicago River
Stanton Park
Seward Park
North Park Ave.
Sedgwick St.
N. Hudson Ave.
N. Orleans St.
N. Franklin St.
N. LaSalle St.

Historical Society

start here

finish here

Church

Germania Club
1. Germania Club
2. Moody Memorial Church
3. Frame cottages
4. Crilly Court
5. 315 and 319 West Eugenie Street
6. Twin Anchors Tavern
7. Walter A. Netsch, Jr. House
8. Anton Franzen House
9. St. Michael's Church
10. 554 West Eugenie Street
11. Steel and Glass House
12. Raised sidewalk
13. The White House
14. Steppenwolf
15. Yondorf Hall
16. Piper's Alley
17. The Second City
18. Zannies
19. West Burton Place
20. Cobbler Square
21. Oscar Mayer Company
22. The House of Gluntz
23. 1211 North La Salle

3. **frame cottages.** These one- and two-story homes went up sometime between 1871 and 1874, when a tough new city building ordinance outlawed the further construction of wooden houses. Notice how the plainness of the home's original trim and design shines through the well-turned contemporary restorations; these were once simple worker's houses. Also note the unusually high basements, which rise several feet above street level.

Across the street, occupying an entire block, is a residential complex known as:

4. **Crilly Court.** Begun by Daniel F. Crilly after 1885, Crilly Court contained both housing and commercial space that was geared to people of varying economic means. The interior court itself, where Crilly cut a lane and named it for himself, offered cottages to working families on the lower end of the economic ladder. These well-maintained row houses and apartments possess great charm owing to their partially sequestered location and their appearance, which suggests something of an old "quarter" in New Orleans.

Check out two more vintage cottages up the street:

5. **315 and 319 West Eugenie Street.** These two homes are also examples of wooden dwellings built in the years immediately following the Great Fire. They are noteworthy for their slightly more fanciful exterior trim work, by no means rare even in poor immigrant neighborhoods, where so many skilled artisans made their homes.

At the corner of Eugenie and Sedgwick streets is the:

6. **Twin Anchors Tavern.** This somewhat typical neighborhood watering hole was one of the first sports bars in the city. The ribs at the Twin Anchors are also a draw. Among the famous clientele who've dropped in to sample the fare is none other than Old Blue Eyes himself—crooner Frank Sinatra.

Two short blocks west at the corner, 1700 North Hudson Avenue, is the home of a contemporary architect generally known for his work on a larger scale, the:

7. **Walter A. Netsch, Jr. House.** Netsch, once a partner at the mega-architectural firm of Skidmore, Owings & Merrill, designed the Air Force Academy Chapel and the ultra-modern University of Illinois at Chicago campus, which now occupies the land just west of the Loop where many Hull House Settlement buildings once stood. For his own home (1974), he followed a tradition once favored in Europe during the Middle Ages, in which the orientation of one's domestic space turns inward, away from the street. The house is said to have a central loft that rises 33 feet, and by day, gets light and heat from skylights equipped with passive solar panels.

A brief detour to 1726 North Hudson Avenue reveals an interesting example of the cottages built just after the 1874 building ordinance, the:

8. Anton Franzen House. If there is such a thing as a representative Chicago house, then this cottage is the classic type. Frank Lloyd Wright's original Oak Park cottage was not so different in appearance from this demure story-and-a-half, with its broad gabled facade. The distinguishing feature of the Franzen House, built in 1880, is the fact of its brick—rather than wood—construction.

On the square at the end of Eugenie Street is the monumental:

9. St. Michael's Church. Throughout the early to mid-19th century, the two major branches of the Roman Catholic Church in America were the Irish and the German. Several features distinguished these nationality-based practitioners from each other. In general, the German church, predominantly Bavarian, was somewhat more mystical and more expansive in its liturgy, while the Irish church was more rational and puritanical. Since the majority of German immigrants to America were Protestants, the German wing of the Catholic church was perpetually under the authority of an Irish-dominated hierarchy. Nonetheless, the German national parishes were allowed a fair degree of autonomy in preserving their unique liturgical practices and in the observance of any culturally determined feastdays. The feast of Corpus Christi, for example, brought forth a level of pageantry among German Catholics that was unknown among the Irish.

In time, such differences were leveled—though even to this day in the more remote backwaters of the Midwest not entirely extinguished—and the national parishes lost much of their culturally homogeneous character. Looking at St. Michael's, however, one can easily conjure up an image of ceremonial grandeur to match the scale on which this fine and massive Romanesque temple was created.

Within the church, the southern European influence is also keenly felt in the elaborate baroque appointments. Here, as if guarding the vaults that lead to heaven, the patron spirit, an effigy of the angel Michael, hovers over the faithful. In the iconography of Catholicism, this saint, who drove the proud and disobedient Adam and Eve from Paradise, exercises a powerful position. "St. Michael the Archangel, defend us in battle against the wickedness and snares of the devil . . ." This final plea at the end of every mass during the days of the old Tridentine liturgy was one of the few spoken in English before the sweeping reforms of Vatican II replaced Latin with the vernacular.

Crossing the great apron that spans the courtyard before the entrance to St. Michael's, we again pick up Eugenie Street and move on to one of the more unusual homes in the neighborhood:

10. 554 West Eugenie Street. As you stand before this oddly appealing edifice, it is not immediately obvious exactly what you are looking at. Is it a futuristic house of worship? A snappy commercial building? A nest of avant-garde domestic flats? Two semi-attached homes? Suspended between two apparently separate structures is a belfry, housing a molded object whose geometric shape must certainly owe something to the influence of the Prairie School. Nor is this the only reverberation from past architectural styles patched throughout the exterior form of this 1991 postmodern fantasy, which, somewhat anticlimactically, turns out to be a single family dwelling after all. The tower, incidentally, pays homage to its counterpart at neighboring St. Michael's.

Turn north on Larabee Street. An unusual dwelling at the end of this block at no. 1949, near Armitage, is known as the:

11. Steel and Glass House. Built in 1949 (though thoroughly revamped 30 years later), this home represents the post–World War II architecture of optimism at its most daring. The steel-framed house, wrapped in glass around 5,000 square feet of interior space, looks suspiciously at first like one of those modified-Miesian grade schools that popped up everywhere in the United States throughout the 1950s. Much of the beguilingly attractive interior, however, can be viewed from the outside— such is the price paid by those who live in glass houses—and this softens considerably one's initial impression of something cold and institutional.

Double back to Willow Street and continue west until reaching Halsted. As you will have noticed by now during our brief stroll, this section of Old Town in particular is a genuine architectural showcase. There are many princely homes among the troll-like pillbox row houses and suburban-style garden apartments that make you keep looking over your shoulder for signs of the nearest shopping mall. Well, we can't deliver the mall, but a bonafide entertainment and nightlife strip, interwoven with many tony boutiques as well, looms on the horizon. The Halsted strip, with its host of power shops and restaurants (Banana Republic, The Gap, Café Ba-Ba-Reeba!, Carlucci's—to drop just a few of the more recognizable names) trails off beyond Old Town to the north, running from Willow Street to Fullerton and beyond. File this away for future reference, because our path takes us in the opposite direction.

As we walk down Halsted toward North Avenue, there are several landmarks to point out along the way. First is the:

12. raised sidewalk in front of 1713 North Halsted. This is a rare relic of the generally seamless transformation of the urban landscape from one epoch to the next. The roadway was raised, and the old house remained down in the hollow.

REFUELING STOP Drop into **Pizza Capri,** 1733 N. Halsted, near Willow one block above North Avenue (tel. 280-5700). Try a slice of one of their specialty pizzas, like Thai pie or veggie twist, or select from a menu that includes pasta dishes, salads, and milk and cookies.

Across the street, at 1700 North Halsted, is a building I heard referred to as simply:

13. The White House. This relic of ersatz elegance may indeed have once housed the upper-echelon bordello that local legend subscribes to it.

Next down the block at 1650 North Halsted is the reigning off-Loop Theater of Chicago:

14. Steppenwolf. Actually, Steppenwolf, which began as a shoe-string operation nurtured by the artistic capital of its associated actors, directors, and supporters, has risen in recent years to the ranks of the few regional theaters that can lay claim to national prominence.

On the corner of Halsted at 758 West North Avenue is a large building housing a bank, but formerly known as:

15. Yondorf Hall. In general, the German-American community was so club-minded that privately developed commercial halls provided entrepreneur builders with viable investment opportunities, so great was the ongoing demand for meeting space. It was not unusual for some active male members of the German-American community to hold membership simultaneously in three or four lodges, singing clubs, or other political or religious fraternal societies, attending weekly meetings decked out in the appropriate regalia of each organization. The Yondorf Building, built in 1887, contained six separate halls. The principle one, a vast hall on the third floor equipped with a stage and gallery, remains empty today, partially renovated but still largely in possession of its period character and charm. The hall is not open to the public, and what plans exist for its continued restoration and utilization remain shrouded in corporate secrecy.

From this vantage point on the corner of Halsted and North Avenue, there are several points of interest to call to your attention. A block to your west, Clybourn Avenue crosses North Avenue. This is the beginning of the so-called Clybourn Corridor, a district filled with old red-brick manufactures formerly

TURNVATER JAHN AND THE TURNER MOVEMENT

In 1811, Friedrich Ludwig Jahn founded a gymnastic society in a suburb of Berlin that would ultimately evolve into a worldwide popular movement for physical education and fitness. Jahn's initial purpose was political: He hoped to encourage young men to prepare themselves through exercise, military drill, and patriotic fervor to expel the French, who had occupied much of Germany under Napoleon. What began as outdoor calisthenics soon moved indoors, as Jahn developed a program of gymnastics based on his invention of the parallel bars, the rings, the balance beam, the horse, and the horizontal bars.

By 1819, Jahn's movement had spread rapidly throughout Germany, and—with its social democratic leanings—came to be viewed as a threat to the ruling oligarchy. Like Socrates, Jahn was seen as a corrupter of youths. The movement was banned, and Jahn was imprisoned for a year then exiled to a small Prussian village where he could be removed from contact with university and secondary-level students, who had formed the backbone of the radical gymnastic clubs.

Later, many of those radical youths, after participating in the failed Revolution of 1848, immigrated to the United States, carrying their experience in the Turner (German for "gymnast") Movement with them as part of their cultural baggage. By the 1880s, at least 200 Turnvereins had been established in the United States, concentrated for the most part in the German Belt of the Midwest.

German-American culture, highly visible well into the 20th century, suffered a severe setback with the outbreak of World War I. From that point forward, the Turner Clubs, like the many German-language schools, fraternal societies, churches, and newspapers, either disappeared entirely or rapidly assimilated to the mainstream of American culture. Jahn himself, the founding father of gymnastics, though a forgotten figure in American historical memory, retains a shadowy presence in many cities, in the form of public monuments. In Chicago, his statue stands in Humboldt Park on the city's northwest side, and he remains the obscure namesake of the northside Friedrich Ludwig Jahn Public School, near the hip nightlife and blues club district off Belmont Avenue.

employed by light industry; the area is rapidly being transformed into a mixed residential and entertainment zone to include some very hot nightlife spots and restaurants. Below North Avenue, a German-style eatery from the old immigrant days called the Golden Ox Restaurant remains at 1578 North Clybourn Avenue as does the old Mozart Hall at no. 1534. Bub City, patterned after restaurateur Richard Melman's fantasy of a Texas road-house, serves up savory Cajun platters just off Clybourn Avenue at 901 West Weed Street. A bit farther up Clybourn Avenue at no. 1960 is Bossa Nova, a super spot featuring world music and mouth-watering tapas. Somewhat closer, but still several blocks above North Avenue is our recommended spot for refreshment.

REFUELING STOP   It's a bit of a stretch, and going away from the direction of our continuing tour, but the **Goose Island Brewing Co.,** 1800 North Clybourn Avenue (tel. 915-0073), is worth the effort. The only drawback is that once you've discovered the Goose Island Brewery, you may never get back to the walking tour. The two main draws here are the food—like the jalapeño chicken soup and the many delicious appetizers and sandwiches—and the beer, brewed on the premises in 30 spectacular varieties, only a half dozen of which are available in any given season. Goose Island also consumes about 3,000 pounds of potatoes a week making the best chips you can imagine, served up gratis.

Our tour continues at Wells Street, Old Town's main drag, approximately half a mile to the east. To get there from Halsted, you have three options. You can hail a cab, if you're so inclined and lucky; you can hop the North Avenue bus; or you can walk. At a brisk pace you can cover the ground quickly, as there's nothing much to see on this strip. But this is the area I mentioned at the beginning of the tour, where you must exercise a bit of caution, since the fringe of the neighborhood here is somewhat marginal.

On the northwest corner of North Avenue at 1608 North Wells Street, is:

16. Piper's Alley. Saints be praised; there is a shopping mall in Old Town. The complex of commercial spaces was the site of a former bakery owned by Henry Piper in 1880, and Old Town's most popular tourist attraction during the 1960s, filled with boutiques and head shops. Today it is still home to the cinema, facing North Avenue, that hosts the annual Chicago Film Festival, and, at another entrance at 1616 North Wells Street, that infamous bawdy house:

17. The Second City. Since the mid-'50s, the hothouse humor of Chicago has become the mainstream humor of the nation. It began with Mike Nichols and Elaine May, who gained their spurs in Chicago at clubs like The Second City, then won a national audience on the airwaves of early television with biting psycho-satires saddled to the traditional skit-based humor of vaudeville. This was Lenny Bruce with dentures. Nichols and May plated their sarcasm with cynical smiles; they were seldom vulgar and never overtly subversive like Lenny. Many great stars have since followed the tightrope path these two had blazed. Among the names of their spiritual protégés who've played this club are Robert Klein, John Belushi, Dan Ackroyd, Bill Murray, John Candy, and Robin Williams. Who's next? You'll have to go to the Improv session after the show to find out.

Cut in the same pattern is another club down the block, just south of North Avenue at 1548 North Wells Street:

18. Zannies. The routines here are well polished, having proven themselves before national audiences on *The Tonight Show, Late Night with David Letterman,* HBO, Showtime, and so forth.

An unusual constellation of homes is our next point of interest on:

19. West Burton Place. On the Wells Street side, the short block, formerly called Carl Street, is entered by way of the Burton Place outdoor mall. Many of these buildings were once standard Victorian homes of the cookie-cutter variety that have since been remodeled beyond recognition into multidwelling apartment buildings. The remodeling, moreover, had the force of an artistic statement, the collaborative effort of many hands, but the inspiration of two men, Sol Kagen and Edgar Miller, who had studied together in 1917 at the School of the Art Institute. The gist of their visions could be summed up as handyman rehabs with salvaged and found materials. Today, leases on apartments like those in 155 West Burton Place, considered Miller's masterpiece, are preciously guarded. As for 151 West Burton Place, try to unravel the steps it took to alter the old Victorian outline of this house into the charming art deco form of its contemporary exterior.

There is another interesting example of Edgar Miller's work on the next block, at 154 West Schiller Street.

Between Schiller and Evergreen at 1350 North Wells Street is another mall of sorts with interesting historical roots, mixing residential and commercial uses:

20. Cobbler Square. Roughly 20 existing buildings were welded together to form this post-modern confection. The oldest piece of the pie, dating from 1880, was the assembly plant of a bicycle manufacturer called Western Wheel Works. That factory was then purchased in 1911 by the legendary William M. Scholl. Yes, Virginia, there was a real Dr. Scholl, and he founded his foot care accessory business right here on Wells Street. Some of today's retail tenants include a branch of Barbara's Bookstore, and the fashion boutiques of Chicago Originals, Possessions, and Fashion Station. Most of the other tenants live here in some 295 residential units.

Besides Dr. Scholl, Old Town had another large business whose wares are household words throughout America, a plant manufacturing the meat products of the:

21. Oscar Mayer Company. As you walk down Wells Street, look west along Scott Street. Those red-brick factory buildings you see were the headquarters of the well-known meat-packing firm until 1992, when this branch of the company was finally shut down, and all operations moved to greener pastures. How these buildings will be used in the future, if at all, is anybody's guess.

There's an odd duck of a retail store close to Division Street at 1206 North Wells Street:

22. The House of Gluntz. This famous Old Town wine emporium dates from 1888, when a farmer from Westphalia decided to settle in the city and change his profession. During Prohibition, Gluntz managed to stay afloat by selling altar wine and products used for manufacturing wines at home. Today, The House of Gluntz is one of the most respected wine merchants in Chicago. Wine-tasting events are held here periodically, including an annual fall tasting of rare and fine madeiras. If the store is open and the owner willing, take a look at the collection of old bottles, glasses, and cooper's tools in the store's museum room.

Our final stop takes us two blocks east along Division Street to:

23. 1211 North La Salle. Mural artist Richard Haas's trompe l'oeil paintings on the facades of public and private buildings, here and in Europe, have encouraged a welcome national trend to liven up the American urban landscape. You can hardly go to an American city and not see a detailed, hyper-realist program of windows, or a cartoon facade of a textbook classical temple painted on what was formerly the blank wall of some boring downtown building. This particular sample of Haas's handiwork, literally covering the walls of a converted apartment building from head to foot, is really a crown jewel of the genre. He calls this work *Homage to the Chicago School of Architecture*. The eye-catching centerpiece, facing Division Street, is the reproduction of Sullivan's *Golden Doorway* from the Transportation Building of the 1891 World's Columbian Exhibition.

WALKING TOUR 9

Hyde Park

Start: 53rd Street and Lake Park Avenue, across from the 53rd Street stop of the Metra train.

Public Transportation: Take the METRA, Chicago's suburban train line, from one of two downtown locations, Randolph at Michigan Avenue and Van Buren at La Salle Street. Known locally as the IC—for the Illinois Central the METRA line replaced—take the South Chicago train; the ride to 53rd Street takes about 15 minutes. Another option is the much more frequently running no. 6 Jeffrey Express bus, which you can pick up at designated stops in the Loop along State Street.

Finish: The Museum of Science and Industry in Jackson Park.

Time: 2 to 3 hours.

Best Times: Daylight hours, seven days a week.

Worst Times: After dark.

Before the mid-1800s, the land now occupied by Hyde Park was only sparsely settled. Farmsteads, a roadhouse or two, an outlying estate belonging to some squire seeking pastoral relief from the foul odors and anarchy of the city: This then was the landscape of human habitats in an area located, according to today's urban measure, a mere 50 or 60 city blocks below the southern bounds of contemporary downtown Chicago.

As an official entity, Hyde Park wasn't founded until 1853, when a young lawyer, Paul Cornell, transplanted to the Midwest from New York, purchased 300 acres here along the lakefront as a speculative real estate investment. Cornell's vision was to create a genteel haven, near the city, for gentle folk of means who, like himself, made their way in life as professionals and executives. He chose the name "Hyde Park" because he admired that Hudson River enclave of the same name back East; it was the kind of village he hoped to replicate on these southern shores of Lake Michigan.

Cornell's intention from the beginning was to attract a large institution that would provide a firm base for the local economy, but to keep all forms of heavy industry and manufacture at bay. To a large degree, Hyde Park's development has proceeded according to Cornell's plan ever since. There have been bumps and grinds along the way, but Hyde Park today remains one of the most desirable residential neighborhoods in the world within the actual confines of a great metropolis—that is, one even remotely approximating the size and complexity of the city of Chicago.

The institution Cornell dreamed of didn't materialize in Hyde Park until after his death, but it was the establishment of the University of Chicago in 1890 which, more than any single factor, made the fulfillment of his dream possible, even in the modified form it has assumed today. Hyde Park over the years has been much buffeted by a succession of changing social realities: What was originally an elite neighborhood in the Age of Innocence, has today become solidly middle class . . . and racially integrated. Ultimately, it was this social compromise in the area of race relations that allowed Hyde Park to preserve its privileged ambience, when, by the end of World War II, the "white flight" to the suburbs was transforming neighborhoods all over Chicago's south side into racially homogeneous ghettos, as more and more African Americans, displaced from the rural communities of the South, fled north in search of blue-collar employment.

Hyde Park had retained its relatively uniform character as an affluent neighborhood until roughly the 1890s, when its Jackson Park was selected as the site for the World's Columbian Exposition. Against the wishes of the villagers, Hyde Park was then incorporated into the city of Chicago, and the massive development that accompanied the creation of the Exposition, plus the ongoing advances and spread of public transportation, made it possible and convenient for middle- and working-class families to take up residence there.

By World War II, the village was in decline, but the powerful presence of the University of Chicago, a massive injection of Federal funds in the form of an urban renewal program that would become a model for cities all over the country, and the decision to no longer block middle-class African Americans who wished to live there, allowed Hyde Park to survive as a serene and self-contained college town, surrounded by some of the poorest and most troubled neighborhoods in Chicago.

Our tour begins just up the block from the IC train station at 1518 East 53rd Street, a famous Hyde Park institution:

1. **Valois.** Pronounced "va-*loys*" rather than "val-*wa*," this steam-table cafeteria has its roots as a working-man's eatery, but for years has also held a strong appeal among college students and other residents of varied social backgrounds. Shoulder to shoulder, you will see the bank president here chowing down with the plumber. Valois has the status in Hyde Park to deserve special mention as a point of interest, but it should also obviously be considered as our initial Refueling Stop in the neighborhood.

Our next stop is a complex of shops, studios, and restaurants with historic roots in Hyde Park's bohemian and avant-garde art movement:

2. **Harper Court.** Many of the buildings where a colorful constellation of Hyde Park artists once lived and had their studios were demolished during the massive urban renewal that took place here during the 1950s. As a form of compensation, Harper's Court was built to "support artisans, craftsmen, and other services of special cultural or community significance." In general, rents at Harper's Court would prove too high for struggling artists to afford. But four buildings were constructed around a pleasant public square, and are occupied by retail tenants whose rents generate income that benefits some artists and the community in general. Among the specialty items featured in the boutiques are beads, goods from Africa, security hardware, health food, and futons. There's also a gourmet carry out, a café, a Japanese restaurant, and a branch of a popular northside Chicago restaurant called Medici.

Now cross 53rd Street and enter Blackstone Avenue. On the west side of the street, near the corner of 54th Street are several:

3. **workers' cottages.** These dwellings are typical of the homes built for workers who came to reside in Hyde Park, where they built, ran, and maintained the halls and attractions of the World's Columbian Exposition in the early 1890s.

Return to 53rd Street and continue west along the south side of the street. Pause on the southeast corner of Dorchester Avenue and look across the large lot to the:

4. **oldest house in Hyde Park.** The lean-to or shed-like structure at the rear of the home at 5317 South Dorchester Avenue was originally a board-and-batten sided cottage, built by

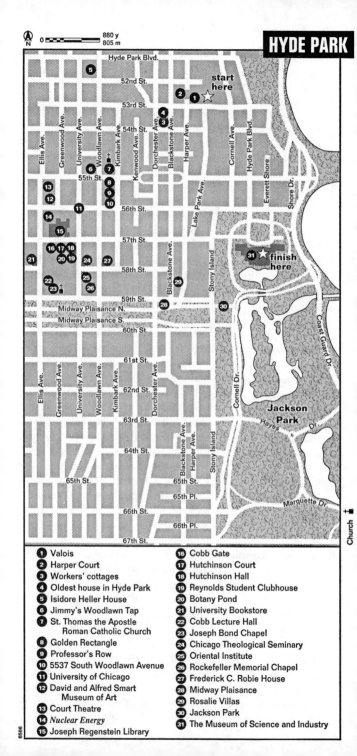

HYDE PARK

0 [scale] **880 y**
805 m

Hyde Park Blvd.

52nd St.

start here ⭐

53rd St.

54th St.

55th St.

56th St.

57th St.

58th St.

finish here ⭐

59th St.

Midway Plaisance N.
Midway Plaisance S.

60th St.

61st St.

62nd St.

63rd St.

64th St.

65th St.

65th St.

65th Pl.

66th St.

66th Pl.

67th St.

Ellis Ave.
Greenwood Ave.
University Ave.
Woodlawn Ave.
Kimbark Ave.
Kenwood Ave.
Dorchester Ave.
Blackstone Ave.
Harper Ave.
Cornell Ave.
Hyde Park Blvd.
Lake Park Ave.
Everett Shore
Shore Dr.

Blackstone Ave.
Stony Island

Jackson Park

Cornell Dr.
Hayes Dr.
Coast Guard Dr.

Marquette Dr.

Church ⛪

6566

Henry C. Work in approximately 1859. Work, incidentally, was a very popular composer around the time of the Civil War, and a writer of temperance songs.

Our next attraction takes us a bit off the main trail of our tour, but a detour and some extra walking are decidedly worthwhile when the quarry is a home built by Frank Lloyd Wright. Walk four blocks west to Woodlawn Avenue, turn right or north, and continue just across 52nd Street to 5132 South Woodlawn Avenue, the:

5. **Isidore Heller House.** Here is living proof that by 1897, when this home was completed, Wright's reputation had already soared sufficiently in Chicago to attract important commissions outside Oak Park, which was, until then, the incubator of his art. Even as early as 1897, when not restrained by the limits imposed by the existing structures he was often called upon by Oak Park neighbors to remodel or renovate, Wright already demonstrates with Heller House a full command of the Prairie School idiom, so well-fermented by that time in the minds of the Young Turk architects of Chicago, with Wright very much in the forefront.

For Wright, the flat roofs and exaggerated horizontality of the Heller House design, were much more than an aesthetic statement; with a zealot's impatience, he was already aggressively about the business of trimming from the modern home all the useless space that smacked of Victorian excess, of form without function. Those bands of windows on Heller House, for example, were not only bold and attractive, they brought in an abundance of natural light; and yet, with their placement under low, extended eves, Wright also managed to preserve a sense of domestic privacy. With Heller House, Wright also employs the hidden entrance—a trademark of this and many subsequent Wright designs—which he felt was more seemly and discreet than a front door fully exposed to the world.

Now return along Woodlawn Avenue to 1152 East 55th Street:

6. **Jimmy's Woodlawn Tap.** If the University of Chicago had an equivalent of the Yale "Whiffenpoof Song," Jimmy's Woodlawn Tap would occupy the honored place of "Maury's Tavern." Jimmy's is U. of C.'s main hangout, indeed it's the only tavern remaining from Hyde Park's golden era before urban renewal obliterated a host of other gin mills where the old college crowd used to entertain itself. But as traditional college bars go, Jimmy's fits the archetype to a "T." The labyrinth of separate rooms are appropriately dark and grungy; there are always a few hard-core regulars perched at the bar popping shots and chasers; and the students fill the booths between classes quaffing drafts and eating burgers.

Return one block east, and just in from the corner at 55th Street is 5472 South Kimbark Avenue:

7. St. Thomas the Apostle Roman Catholic Church. This house of worship gets a fair amount of attention from architecture buffs for two reasons. First off, it doesn't look like a conventional Catholic church, but architect Barry Byrne's 1924 design is highly regarded nonetheless; and second, Byrne served an apprenticeship with Frank Lloyd Wright, and the influence of the Prairie School is evident in much that is unique about St. Thomas. The entryway in particular, a double curtain of delicate, highly ornamented terra-cotta, is definitely the Wright stuff, or more accurately, reflects those influences of lyrical design that Wright picked up from his own Svengali, Louis Sullivan.

As we cross 55th Street and head south, we are entering an area known as the:

8. Golden Rectangle. In Hyde Park, this is real estate heaven, a few blocks bordering the University of Chicago campus containing the neighborhood's priciest and most desirable housing.

Among the most elegant of these dwellings are several clusters of row houses wrapping around Kimbark Avenue, and running down 56th Street to the next block, Woodlawn, and known as:

9. Professor's Row. In this group are included 5558 South Kimbark Avenue and 1220–1222, 1226, 1228 and 1234 East 56th Street. These homes were built collectively by several members of the university faculty, one of whose brother was the chief architect. In appearance, there's something very proper and staid about these houses, like gentlemen in morning suits attending a society wedding. Their landmark tile roofs, however, were the subject of a somewhat pedestrian controversy in recent years, having been selected by migrating parrots from South America as a preferred nesting spot. Once the birds took up residence, they seemed to lose all further interest in returning south. Local wildlife partisans screamed "fowl" when the homeowners, allied with Illinois farmers who claimed the birds were a danger to crops, attempted to evict the intruders by force.

At the corner, turn back to see:

10. 5537 South Woodlawn Avenue. One of the great minds of modern nuclear science, Enrico Fermi, once lived here with his family while working on the Manhattan Project and later as a member of the research faculty of the University of Chicago. Fermi was the 1938 recipient of the Nobel Prize for Physics; under the pretext of going to Stockholm to receive his prize, he and his family fled Italian fascism and settled in the United States.

During the next portion of our excursion, we will selectively tour the campus buildings of the:

11. **University of Chicago.** In a recent column, George Will quipped that, in the ranking of fun schools, the University of Chicago comes in last. And it is certainly a fact that "Chicago" has a reputation for cerebral seriousness that surpasses virtually all other institutes of higher learning in the United States. Just look at the list of U. of C. faculty, past and present, who've won the Nobel Prize—over threescore, and the count seems to increase each year.

   John D. Rockefeller, on behalf of the American Baptist Society, founded the University in 1890, on land donated and purchased from Chicago merchant prince Marshall Field. It's certainly no wonder, given this trio of progenitors, that the University has since provided a comfortable haven for some of the most celebrated "conservatives," such as Milton Friedman and Allan Bloom, to strut through the American academic scene in the 20th century. For the most part, however, it would not be fair to characterize the U. of C. as either too liberal or too conservative. Few schools anywhere put a higher premium on getting to the truth that lies beyond the cant of all competing ideologies. Here the Socratic method survives, embodied in the sentiments urged upon a recent class of incoming freshmen: "If some one asserts it, deny it; if some one denies it, assert it."

   Henry Ives Cobb, a leading practitioner of the Romanesque architecture still fashionable in the 1890s, was commissioned to provide a master plan in Gothic for the U. of C. campus, because the university trustees felt that style more suitable to an institution rooted in the more recent religious traditions of the West. Cobb rose to the occasion; he imagined two sets of quadrangles facing each other across a common green, where the buildings formed exterior ramparts, broken by gates and portals, the ultimate effect not unlike a walled medieval monastery, or indeed, an English university. With some modification, this is essentially what the core of the U. of C. campus came to resemble, making it one of the most idyllic settings for higher education in the country. One can be forgiven a pang of envy, when strolling the interior quads of this grand campus, toward those privileged enough to study here.

   Since we are now on 56th Street, we'll delay entering the campus proper for a moment, and take in several of the newer buildings just north of this street and the main quads. Our first stop is the:

12. **David and Alfred Smart Museum of Art.** This complex of galleries houses the extensive University of Chicago art collection, located within the larger Cochrane-Woods Art Center at

5550 South Ellis Avenue. The museum bears the names of its principal patrons, the two brothers who founded *Esquire* magazine. This large, square structure was envisioned as the core of a new arts quadrangle and "student village with athletic facilities, housing, and a café," an ambitious plan that, thus far, has yet to materialize. The museum's permanent collection contains over 5,000 works ranging from classical antiquity to the contemporary; but the curators' emphasis is on a program of frequently changing exhibitions around such intriguing themes as "Art of the Mentally Ill" and "Fear of Women in Late Nineteenth Century Art." In the courtyard of the Art Center is the Vera and A. D. Elden Sculpture Garden, with Henry Moore's "reclining figure" as its centerpiece.

Behind the Cochrane-Woods Art Center, at 5535 South Ellis Avenue is the:

13. Court Theatre. This is a very attractive, professionally outfitted theatrical space, used by the university theater department to stage its well-regarded productions.

Now cross 56th Street and walk south on Ellis Avenue, toward the main campus. On the east side of the street, about a third of the way down the block, look for:

14. *Nuclear Energy.* This 1967 abstract sculpture by Henry Moore marks the spot where the world's first controlled nuclear chain reaction occurred on December 2, 1942. Enrico Fermi headed the team that accomplished this historic feat with an atomic pile installed in a squash court under what was then Stagg Stadium. Today, a new, massive complex dominates this site, the:

15. Joseph Regenstein Library. The architect for this act of "concrete brutalism," as one of his critics has uncharitably characterized the design, was Walter A. Netsch, Jr., whose home is mentioned in our tour of Old Town. Netsch's other major commission in the city, the University of Illinois at Chicago Circle, just a bit south and west of the Loop, is also much denigrated by critics and, it seems, not well loved by the public either. One never hears a good word about this campus of concrete slabs, the model for which seems to have been that South American moonscape, Brasília, the prefab capital of Brazil. To say that the Regenstein Library sticks out like a sore thumb, and indeed clashes with practically every other building on the U. of C. campus, would not be an overstatement—nor one that isn't shared by many U. of C. alumni.

From here, the architectural landscape soars to a higher plane, one unabashedly traditional in every respect, radiating an atmosphere of other-worldliness and well-being that is completely appropriate to the work of scholarship. We will enter the main campus on 57th Street, between Ellis and University avenues, by way of:

16. Cobb Gate. Soon before he was replaced as campus architect in 1901, Henry Ives Cobb, designed and constructed this highly ornamental gate at his own expense. This work demonstrated his commitment to the Gothic detailing with which he adorned practically every building whose construction he supervised, before budget cutbacks put an end to these expensive decorations. The "grotesques," the mythic figures climbing to the tip of the gate's pointed gable, have come to represent an allegory of undergraduate progress. According to one account in a University of Chicago publication, "The largest figures, at the base of the eves on either side, are said to be the admissions counselor and college examiner defying ready passage. Above them are the first-year college students with tenuous academic grip, about to lose their footing. The second-year students, with firmer grasp and heads erect, scurry ahead. Snarling at the second-year students to keep them at a respectful distance, the third-year students strain to reach the top. The fourth-year students, having mastered the slippery slope, stand proudly at the educational pinnacle."

To the immediate east of Cobb Gate is a loggia, a roofed arcade or passageway. Cross through it to:

17. Hutchinson Court. An English sunken garden provides the model for this stone-paved courtyard, the site of formal receptions, recitals, student gatherings, and outdoor performances of various kinds. Hutchinson Court was designed by John Olmsted, son of Frederick Law Olmsted, the great landscape architect who had come to Chicago to supervise the redesign of Jackson Park for the World's Columbian Exposition.

Enclosing Hutchinson Court is a group of interconnected buildings known as the Tower Group. Mitchell Tower, which anchors this corner of the quad, was inspired by a similar bell tower at Magdalen College at Oxford University in England. The tower contains the Palmer chimes, named for the first woman dean at the university and installed in 1908. They are used in the ancient English art of change ringing, in which the bells are rung in every possible order and permutation, creating a din that is not universally applauded by residents, on campus or off.

To the left of Mitchell Tower is:

18. Hutchinson Hall. Walking inside this former men's dining hall, you feel as if you've entered into a scene from *Tom Brown's School Days*. The spirit of the British Public School is alive and well at the University of Chicago. In this 115-foot-long, but relatively narrow room, the cathedral-high, hammer-beamed ceiling, the raised oak-paneled walls, the arched and leaded windows, and the oversized fireplaces all contribute to an unmistakably British atmosphere of a by-gone era. Hutchinson Hall now provides its anachronistic seating for a cafeteria, open to all.

To the right of Mitchell Tower is the:

19. Reynolds Student Clubhouse. Also built originally for the male students, the club once contained various rooms for recreational activities, like billiards and bowling, as well as a library and reading room. Echos of historicism also dominate the architecture of this building, the grand central staircase in the entryhall suggesting something of the traditional English manor house. Today Reynolds Club serves as a union for the entire student body, and contains two theatrical spaces, a branch of the campus bookstore, and a small café.

Return now to Hull Court, the area facing Cobb Gate. That ornamental pool of water you see next to the Erman Biology Center is called:

20. Botany Pond. This is also the landscaping work of John Olmsted, who was guided by the science faculty when the pond was formerly stocked with exotic specimens and plants from the botany department. Today, the pond is used for experiments in ecology.

Now continue on to the central rectangle between the two quads and walk to the west, crossing Ellis Avenue to no. 5750, the:

21. University Bookstore. This many-gabled, red-brick building dates from 1902, and was funded directly by John D. Rockefeller specifically to house the University of Chicago Press. After 1971, the building was converted to retail space for the University Bookstore, which sells some very durable sportswear in addition to the many volumes of textbooks and tradebooks.

Now, cross Ellis Avenue again and re-enter the quadrangle, the first building in the South Quad is:

22. Cobb Lecture Hall. On October 1, 1992, when the university received its first class of students, Cobb Hall *was* the University of Chicago, the first of 18 buildings designed by Henry Ives Cobb, and named, not in his honor, but for the unrelated donor of the building, Silas B. Cobb. In the early days, each university department occupying the original second through fourth floors of Cobb Hall was organized around its own classrooms and library. A massive renovation, begun in 1963, completely gutted and transformed the interior of the voluminous structure, which measures 168 feet long and 85 feet wide. Cobb Hall's distinctive Gothic exterior, however, was scrupulously retained in every detail. Directly in front of Cobb Hall's main entrance, is the "C" bench, a gift of the Class of 1903; until the 1960s, only varsity lettermen and their dates could sit there!

Across the courtyard from Cobb Hall is Swift Hall, the Divinity School. Connected to this building in a separate wing by way of a cloister is the:

23. Joseph Bond Chapel. Even the nonbeliever and the iconoclast will shudder in awe and approval when seeing the interior of this inspired showcase of ecclesiastical craftsmanship, which dates from 1926. It's hard to imagine a chapel being more richly or lovingly decorated than this. Charting a course for the architects and other contributors, a professor of the New Testament from the University Divinity School ensured that the gospels' messages would be fully manifest on every available space, etched in both the woodwork and the stained-glass windows. Divine perorations are scrolled across the top of the entrance, while the beatitudes are carved into a frieze above the interior wainscoting. Every niche has its carved figure or form, whether a dove with an olive branch, a angel blowing its horn, or a cluster of allegorical grapes. The leaded windows are a masterpiece of intricacy and grace. The Bond Chapel, with a seating capacity of 300, is diminutive but not tiny, and is a community favorite for weddings and memorial services.

Follow the roadway running through the center of the campus to 5757 South University Avenue to visit the:

24. Chicago Theological Seminary. There are two points of interest in this double-winged complex: The excellent, well-stocked Seminary Co-op Bookstore, and another sanctuary, the Hilton Memorial Chapel, very tiny and very much a jewel in its own right.

Across 58th Street from the seminary is the renowned archeological repository called the:

25. Oriental Institute. Carvings on the bas-reliefs around the main entrance at 1155 East 58th Street depict the meeting of the East, symbolized by a lion, and the West, represented by a bison. The great historical figures and monuments of each civilization are also juxtaposed. From the East, they are the pyramids, the Sphinx, the ruins of Peresopolis, along with Hammurabi of Babylonia (the lawgiver), Darius of Persia, and Thutmose III of Egypt. From the West are Notre Dame and the Parthenon, as well as Herodotus, Alexander, and Caesar. But don't stand at the doorway; take a few minutes to peruse the extraordinary collection of antiquities inside. How often do you have a chance to see the finds from so many world digs all in one place, some of which date from as far back as 9000 B.C.? And don't miss the little gift shop, with some fine and very unusual imported crafts and jewelry from the Middle East.

Now walk along 58th Street to the corner, and turn right, where half a block to the south (essentially behind the Oriental Institute) is the magnificent:

26. **Rockefeller Memorial Chapel.** Folks, this is no chapel; by any measure or account, the Rockefeller "Chapel," raised between 1925 and 1928, is a full-blown church, if not an actual cathedral. The dimensions are imposing: 265 feet long and 120 feet wide, and the height from sidewalk to roofline, 102 feet. The entrance faces 59th Street. Once the chapel stood open 24 hours a day, but University President Hutchins gave this explanation for a policy decision to close the chapel overnight: "Unfortunately, more souls have been conceived at Rockefeller Chapel than have been saved there."

This news may or may not have pleased the chapel's architect, Bertram Grosvenor Goodhue, whose name sounds Puritanical enough to have been a character in a short story by Nathaniel Hawthorne. But Goodhue, as a leading proponent of the Gothic Revival and of the Arts and Crafts Movement, was clearly an aesthetic sensualist. The Arts and Crafts Movement, incidentally, began in Europe in the mid-19th century as a reaction to mass production, and promoted the decorative arts and a return to fine craftsmanship. As for the Gothic content of the chapel's design, Goodhue did not borrow from a single or even a set of existing models for his conception; he began from scratch by reinterpreting Gothic architecture according to its first principles, which he had studied assiduously.

Through his commitment to authenticity, Goodhue managed to achieve a degree of originality that created a sense of novelty, extending to the building's unusual proportions, its irregular shape, and the placement of the massive tower over the eastern transept. Construction techniques were also rigidly traditional: The building is solid masonry, faced with Indiana limestone; arches and buttresses are actually load-bearing, not decorative, and provide true structural support. The walls of the tower alone are eight feet thick.

The chapel is decorated elaborately, both inside and out, and the numerous carvings, sculptures, and inscriptions provide a world view of religion, politics, history, and philosophy. Among the more than 70 statues decorating the exterior walls are 15 life-sized figures of the world's most revered thinkers and holy men placed among the turrets and gable of the south facade, including Abraham, Moses, Zoroaster, Plato, John the Baptist, St. Francis, Luther, and Calvin, with Jesus at the apex. Even Jan Hus, the great pre-Reformation martyr who inspired many of the non-doctrinal Christian sects, like the American Baptists, is there on the west column, alongside the window. Missing in this

THE WORLD'S COLUMBIAN EXPOSITION

The idea of a World's Fair was a novelty created during the 19th century. Prior to the Chicago Exposition, there had only been two such events, first in London in 1851, and next more than three decades later, in Paris in 1889. It was the occasion of the 400th anniversary of Columbus's arrival in America that put the idea of a third World's Fair on the agenda so soon on the heels of the recent Paris exposition. And four American cities competed for the honor of hosting the grand event. It's very hard today to imagine what the Fair meant to Chicagoans of that time, or to Americans in general.

Fortunately, the Chicago Historical Society and the independent Chicago film company, Kartemquin, imagined this question for us, and have captured this historic spectacle in a video co-production through a montage of images and voices from the past. The video is part of an exhibit called "Grand Illusions: Chicago's World Fair of 1893" on display at the Historical Society. The documentation that follows summarizes that video.

The rivalry between New York and Chicago was particularly fierce. "All Chicago has to boast about is grain, lumber, and meat," a New Yorker snorted. The Chicago retort was carried by a Thomas Nast cartoon, commenting on a scandal in New York politics, and captioned, "At least Chicago slaughters and packs its hogs. New York puts them on committees." Architect John Wellborn Root, appointed chief designer for the Fair, was more direct. He stated, "We have more space, more money, and we have the Lake. Why should we here in Chicago not surpass Paris?"

Root's untimely death in 1891 put his partner, Daniel H. Burnham, in charge of planning. And Burnham had big ideas of his own, as his words in later years can testify. "Make no small plans. They have no magic to stir men's blood." Frederick Law Olmsted, called in to undertake the landscaping, at first was skeptical. He saw Jackson Park as "a morass subject to flooding," but nonetheless "admired the characteristic Chicago audacity" to construct the exposition there.

A decision was made to build a dazzling "city of marble," a grand stage set of temporary halls in plaster and steel, classical in design and "perfectly white." For the first time, thanks to the insistence of leaders like Susan B. Anthony, women would have a say in the exhibits and management of an event of this scale. A Woman's Building was to become one of the Fair's most unique and memorable attractions. When the Fair opened on May 1, 1893, the reactions of the press and public were ecstatic. President Grover Cleveland himself presided at the opening ceremonies.

But not all the praise was uniform. The abolitionist and statesman Frederick Douglass remarked that, "Although there are eight million people of African descent, not one of them seems to have been thought worthy of a place in these inaugural ceremonies. The presence of even one of this race would speak more for the moral civilization of the American Republic than all the domes, towers and tourists that adorn the Exposition rounds."

Over the next six months, practically every notable American of the day would make his way to Chicago, to see the great "artistic, mechanical and scientific achievements of the world to date," and to visit the world pavilions of countries from as far away as Japan. The writers among them would ultimately leave a record of their reflection on the Fair. Their words mirror their personalities: Henry Adams is obscure, Theodore Dreiser gushy, Walt Whitman celebratory, and Franz Boas—the great American anthropologist—appropriately academic, confining his remarks to a few dry comments about the ethnographic exhibit he himself had a hand in staging.

There was nothing stodgy, however, about the "Midway," as the Fair's entertainment zone was dubbed. The Ferris wheel was by no means the most popular attraction. A sign on one pavilion beckoned the public to see the "40 Ladies from 40 Nations." In another exotic amusement called "The Streets of Cairo," a dancer known as Little Egypt displayed her "scandalous gyrations."

The Fair, however, was to "end in gloom" without ceremony, according to a local news story, on October 30, 1893, the day after Chicago's mayor, Carter Harrison, was assassinated in his own home by a newsboy. The buildings of the Exposition were not intended to be permanent. A sentiment existed to preserve them, but Daniel Burnham's word's carried the day. "Let it go," he said. "It has to go, so let it go. Let us put it to the torch and burn it down." And that's precisely what happened. It is no wonder that recollections of the World's Columbian Exposition in Chicago often have a dreamlike quality, as if many visitors weren't sure if the "City of Light" had ever really existed.

ecumenical roll call, however, is Mohammed; even in those days, the Prophet of Islam was getting bad press throughout Christendom.

There is so much more to see on the outside that you will need a university guidebook to take it all in. The same applies to the many details to be discovered within the chapel. Here we can highlight only a handful of the interior delights; the unique glazed-tile ceiling 80 feet above you, the masterfully carved organ screen in the rear of the chapel, and above all, the dazzling symphony of stained glass above the altar, to which your attention will return more than once, involuntarily, so powerful is the force and concentration of the light.

Return now to the intersection of Woodlawn Avenue and 58th Street and cross to the northeast corner where you will see the:

27. Frederick C. Robie House. Wright built Robie House in 1906 for a man who manufactured motorcycles and bicycles. And many experts consider Robie House to be Frank Lloyd Wright's supreme achievement in domestic architecture. But the cold manner in which the critics dissect the elements of this dwelling, seen as a perfect abstraction of the Wright's classic "Prairie House," is a key to my somewhat heretical opinion that Robie House was perhaps never a very "livable" space.

Robie House lacks the warmth Wright achieved with so many of his other Prairie School homes, not least of all his own Oak Park cottage, which of course only evolved into an example of that genre over the years as Wright's mastery of the idiom developed. With Robie House, Wright himself had basically arrived at the end of his Prairie School experimentation. The Robie family only lived here for two and a half years, and by 1926 the house was empty, purchased by the Chicago Theological Seminary, not for the structure but for the site where they envisioned future expansion.

For years thereafter, Robie House kicked around in the university system as an annex for classrooms, dormitory space, even a refectory. It was scheduled for demolition in 1957 and only a desperate, last ditch effort by a group of preservation-minded individuals managed to save Robie House from the wrecker's ball. Today the home has been fully restored, inside and out, and houses offices of the U. of C. Alumni Association. When touring Robie House, consider that its intrinsic appeal is less that of a plausible domestic shelter and more that of an artist's exquisite model, a culmination, in the abstract, of the great architect's vision at a point when that vision was about to undergo a major transformation.

Follow 58th Street east to Blackstone Avenue and turn right toward the:

28. **Midway Plaisance.** This elongated green was laid out by Frederick Law Olmsted during the construction of the World's Columbian Exposition to link Jackson and Washington parks, located at opposite ends of the original Hyde Park village boundaries. The Exposition's entertainment zone, centered around the world's first Ferris wheel, was set up here, and thus the term "the midway" came to be associated with carnivals and amusement parks everywhere.

Continue one block east and turn left on Harper Avenue. Here, between 59th and 57th streets, are remnants of Hyde Park's first planned community:

29. **Rosalie Villas.** A developer named Rosalie Buckingham purchased this land in 1883, with plans for a subdivision of 42 houses on spacious lots to create a semi-rural environment. She hired George Pullman's architect, Solon S. Berman, who had just recently completed the building of the Pullman planned community to the south. Many of the cottages Berman and his colleagues constructed remain, in various states of repair, and line both sides of the block.

At 57th Street walk to the east, cross Lake Park Avenue and enter:

30. **Jackson Park.** When first laid out in 1871 by Olmsted and Vaux, the team who designed Central Park in New York City, this was known as South Park. The full plan for the park was not carried out, however, until more than 20 years later in 1895, after Olmsted had returned to Chicago with his sons to help mount the World's Columbian Exposition. By all means explore the park if you are so inclined, but a short walk beyond the point where we entered Jackson Park, is the final stop on our tour of Hyde Park:

31. **The Museum of Science and Industry.** A detailed visit of the museum is contained in Walking Tour 10, "The Museum of Science and Industry."

WALKING TOUR 10

The Museum of Science and Industry

Start: Great Lobby, Museum of Science and Industry, South Lake Shore Drive at 57th Street.

Public Transportation: From downtown Chicago, take the no. 6 Jeffrey Express bus, which stops within a block of the museum. The Howard/Jackson Park A and B trains, and the Lake/Dan Ryan B trains stop at 55th Street. Transfers can be made to the no. 55 Garfield bus, which will take you to the museum. The METRA commuter train has a stop at 57th Street and Lake Park Avenue, a 10-minute walk from the museum.

Finish: Kid's Starway.

Time: 2 to 4 hours.

Best Times: Between Memorial Day and Labor Day, the museum is open from 9:30am to 5:30pm daily. After Labor Day, the museum is open Monday to Friday from 9:30am to 4pm, Saturday and Sunday to 5:30pm. Admission is charged; taking in a showing at the Omnimax Theater is extra. For additional information, call 312/684-1414.

The Museum of Science and Industry did not open until July 1, 1933, but the building housing the exhibits dates from the 1893 World's Columbian Exposition, when it was known as the Palace of Fine Arts and exhibited a spectacular collection of world art. It is the only major structure to have survived the Exposition, and even then it was merely the form and not the content of the classical masterpiece that was preserved.

After 1920, the Field Museum of Natural History, which had occupied the drafty "Palace" since 1894, moved to its new home in Grant Park, and the old building in Jackson Park was slated for demolition. This civic decision came as no great surprise; the building was, in any case, an ersatz affair, a grand illusion in wood, brick, and plaster; it was never meant to be permanent. But Chicagoans had grown fond of this crumbling relic, for it symbolized their moment of international glory. Soon a movement was afoot—spurred by the philanthropist Julius Rosenwald, Chairman of Sears, Roebuck and Co.—to save the old "Palace," or really to reconstruct what amounted to an exact duplicate in that same location.

Rosenwald had come back in 1911 from a visit to the Deutsches Museum in Munich, Germany, and for some years had been involved in plans to create in Chicago an American institution with a similar focus on industrial advancements. His endowment of the museum allowed the reconstruction project, which spanned an 11-year period from 1929 to 1940, to go forward.

The building's original design, by Charles Atwood—who took on the task for his employer, Daniel H. Burnham, after the death of John Wellborn Root—was enthusiastically received by the consortium of New York architects who wielded a certain degree of artistic control over the overall composition of the 1893 World's Fair. Their approval of Atwood's plan bordered on the ecstatic; Saint-Gaudens himself, then the reigning world-class sculptor in America and crony of the great eastern architects, proclaimed Atwood's plan "the finest thing done since the Parthenon." Given this high praise, it is no wonder that Chicagoans, in voting $5 million for the restoration, had insisted that "the exterior would look exactly like it did in 1893."

The "Palace" was virtually stripped to its foundation: Where a shell of mortar and plaster once stood, a building of solid stone rose in its place; the former skylit domes were rebuilt in tile and copper. Only a portion of the steel beams and columns remain from the original framework. The plaster trim and statuary were replaced by stone columns and carved caryatids, duplicating the decorative effects Atwood had initially borrowed from a temple of the Acropolis. The interior, on the other hand, was completely rethought, finished this time not in plaster, but marble, stainless steel, and bronze. Exhibit space was expanded by a six-acre excavation and the creation of a central quadrant with two additional floors. Into the 400,000 square feet of exhibition space housed within this magnificent resurrection of the original Palace of Fine Arts was installed what has become one of the most popular and successful museums of all time.

Our tour of the museum features a selection of the most popular exhibits, beginning in the:

1. **Grand Lobby.** Lining the walls above the columns of the mezzanine are the names of world visionaries of science and philosophy: Aristotle, Euclid, Galileo, Copernicus, Descartes, Leonardo, Lavoisier, Darwin, Pasteur. . . . Here, amidst the spirits of this august company, you purchase your admission tickets. Keep in mind that on Thursdays, general admission is gratis; you must still pay, however, for the Omnimax movie and other special exhibits. The Museum Store is immediately to your left as you enter, while the major exhibition spaces are in rooms off the central lobby.

Enter the first room to your right, and follow the signs to an exhibit entitled:

2. **Communications.** As you will quickly learn, we've come a long way in telecommunications since Alexander Graham Bell demonstrated the first telephone at the nation's 1876 centennial celebration in Philadelphia. Many witnesses to the event were literally stunned by the realization that this invention, almost overnight, would transform the social reality of the entire planet. You may experience some of that same sense of awe at this display of communications advancements currently under development in our leading research labs, spread over 8,000 square feet in this permanent exhibit, which opened in April 1993.

Many of the individual displays here involve some form of interactive participation, and most are deliberately geared to school-age children. From amphitheater seating, for example, in "The World, Live! Theater," you may tune-in, via a variety of satellite and cable feeds, live programming from around the world. Pre-programmed vignettes alternate with the live broadcasts, including one where a music teacher in Chicago coaches, via telecommunications links, her four students from Africa, France, South America, and Los Angeles, enabling them to play ensemble music from these four diverse points of the globe.

The station called "Worldspeak" is educational in another sense for those who are curious about language. By picking up one of 24 headsets, you can hear a child, whose photograph is displayed nearby, greet you in his or her native tongue from one of 24 different parts of the world. The ever-popular "Whispering Gallery" allows two people to stand before parabolic dishes at opposite ends of a large room and whisper audibly to each other, despite the distance between them. And, of course, no preview of communications-to-come would be complete without a futuristic projection or two about how the next generation of computers will alter the realities of our homes, classrooms, and workplaces; several such displays form the core of this exhibit.

By passing through the Communications area toward the West Pavilion, you will come to an exhibit called:

3. Imaging the Tools of Science. By the year 2000, the museum hopes to have installed 60 thematic zones within this exhibit, with an emphasis on interactive involvement. So many outlandish claims are made about the "practical" applications for this or that technological breakthrough, most of which are instantly turned into products that "no home should be without." The classic example remains the personal computer, which continues to sit idle in most homes, while consumers wait for the future benefits—beyond its use as a high-priced version of Nintendo—that this wonder is supposed to bring to their lives. Beyond the workstation, the public—unless self-employed—still can find little domestic use for the personal computer. That's what makes this exhibit so much fun. The potential domestic applications for all these displays of electronic wizardry are next to nil; this is just one big video arcade.

The "virtual reality" station is a real trip, but no one over 18 should attempt to navigate this ride seriously. The coordination and reflexes required to steer yourself through this fascinating obstacle course fade quickly for most humans beyond their teenage years. Here's the situation: You sit at a console, gaze at a screen, and pilot yourself through cityscapes, a canyon, and an electric circuit board—all of which are in constant motion along every imaginable plane. Two companions stand at other panels and manipulate the various environments, throwing a host of roadblocks in your path. I spent my five minutes bouncing off walls, colliding with oncoming traffic, slamming into trees and jagged rocks, and creating electromagnetic havoc on my circuit board. I didn't learn anything, least of all the meaning of "virtual reality"—but I wanted to do it again.

Equally entertaining was the computer graphic station, "Face Net," which functions as a latter-day house of mirrors. A lens transfers your facial image to a computer, which then turns your mug into an electronic version of Mr. Potato Head or the person of a thousand faces. Also about my speed when it comes to science was "The Mystery Lab," pegged to students in grades five through eight, who solve certain lab problems by applying imaging to the forensic method of investigation.

Our next stop, also in the West Pavilion, is a:

4. temporary exhibit space. The museum periodically stages special displays to attract new audiences. In such cases, you pay an additional fee on the spot, if you chose to visit the special exhibit. Particularly popular with museum patrons was the Star

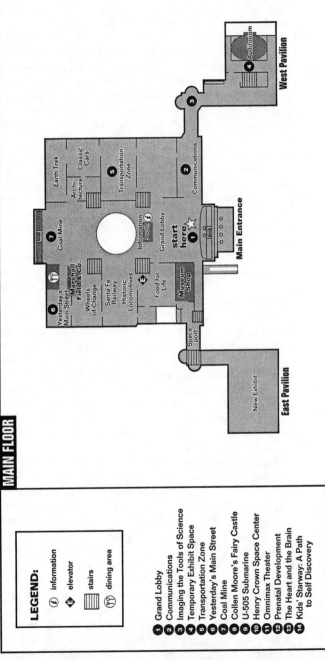

MAIN FLOOR

LEGEND:

- *i* information
- ⬧ elevator
- ▥ stairs
- ⑂ dining area

1. Grand Lobby
2. Communications
3. Imaging the Tools of Science
4. Temporary Exhibit Space
5. Transportation Zone
6. Yesterday's Main Street
7. Coal Mine
8. Collen Moore's Fairy Castle
9. U-505 Submarine
10. Henry Crown Space Center
11. Omnimax Theater
12. Prenatal Development
13. The Heart and the Brain
14. Kids' Starway: A Path to Self Discovery

Main Entrance

start here

Grand Lobby

Information Booth

Museum Shop

Food for Life

Historic Locomotives

Santa Fe Railway

Wheels of Change

Marshall Field & Co.

Yesterday's Main Street

Coal Mine

Earth Trek

Classic Cars

Architecture

Transportation Zone

Communications

West Pavilion

Auditorium

Space-port

East Pavilion

New Exhibit

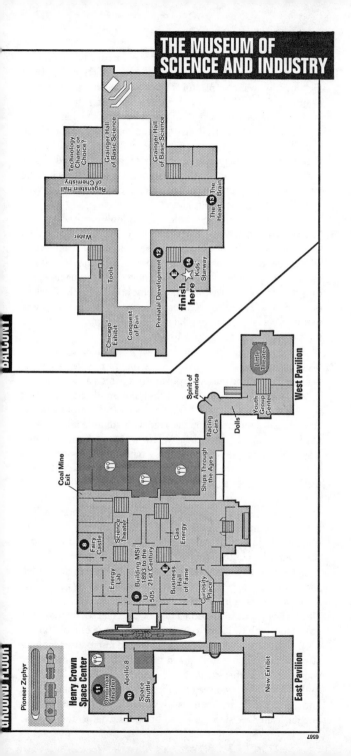

Trek exhibit that was in place during my last visit. While the idea was to demonstrate the science behind science fiction, the gist of the attraction was also playful. The most popular station was the flight deck of the Starship *Enterprise,* where you stood in your circle looking at a full-length image of yourself in a mirror. You then could watch yourself dissolve into molecular vapor as you "beamed" yourself to a sci-fi jungle environment outside the ship. Here your image was re-assembled, and you could "interact" with your surroundings; if you reached out to touch some exotic leaf or an intergalactic critter perched on a rock, they would recede beyond your grasp.

Now return to the central lobby and look for the:

5. **Transportation Zone.** Actually, the whole museum is filled with many artifacts of human transportation. Practically everywhere you turn is some old buckboard, a wood-fired steam locomotive, a stable of classic automobiles, an astronauts' space capsule. One of the newest installations, however, is the fuselage of a genuine 727 jetliner. The craft is cantilevered in such a way that its nose juts out across the exhibit hall; you may go aboard for a closer inspection if you like.

Across the main lobby, at the rear of the building, is:

6. **Yesterday's Main Street.** This is one of the oldest permanent exhibits in the museum, obviously a perennial favorite. The streets you enter are paved with cobblestone and brick. The year is 1910; the city, Chicago. A facade of storefronts recaptures the commercial atmosphere of the era, with some familiar names already in place, like the Walgreen Drug Company and Berghoff's restaurant. The business offices and services you'll pass are also period pieces, appearing as they would have more than eight decades ago: the dentist, the lawyer, the doctor, the dress shop, the post office, the electric company. Several of the businesses are actually operating versions of 1910 stores, including a silent movie house, an ice cream parlor, a branch of Marshall Field & Company, and a studio where you may have your keepsake photo taken.

Right next to Main Street is an even older permanent exhibit, and without exaggeration one of the museum's biggest draws since first opening its doors in 1933, the:

7. **Coal Mine.** This is a reproduction of an actual southern Illinois coal mine, with walls six to eight feet high made of real "Illinois no. 6 seam" coal. You enter the mine's head frame structure via a 50-step stairwell and walk down to an elevator platform, where you board an authentic hoist and descend an additional 50 feet to the shaft. Here you see coal that has been mined and loaded into cars, which are then weighed and emptied into a large hopper, called a "skip," used to bring the coal to the surface.

Next you board a work train, from which you observe a demonstration of both outdated and modern mechanical methods of mining coal. The giant machines seem to be actually cutting into the walls of the shafts, and make a deafening clatter in the process. The visit ends with a bang in the safety room, which you've entered to watch a demonstration on testing for natural gas in mine shafts, the source of many tragic mine explosions if not detected in time.

When you exit the mine, you will already be on the ground floor, where several other popular museum attractions are to be found. But first, you might want to break for some refreshment.

REFUELING STOP The **Century Room** on this level is a self-service cafeteria featuring a health-oriented menu. There are daily specials, like ethnic dishes, stir fries, and meat and vegetable salads. There's a boxed meal for kids, and a wide selection of beverages and desserts from which to choose . . . all reasonably priced.

From the exit of the Century Room, return to the rear of the building, and look for the entrance to:

8. Colleen Moore's Fairy Castle. A silent film star named Colleen Moore created the mother of all dollhouses, a showcase of singular, exquisite miniatures within a fairy castle the size of a small room, which has been on exhibit at the museum since 1949.

Ms. Moore's fascination with dollhouses began when she was two years old; in the subsequent years of her childhood, she collected seven dollhouses, each nicer than the one before. Along the way, her father got her started as a collector of fine miniatures, beginning with an inch-square gilt box, containing a dictionary with words in such fine print they could only be read with the aid of a powerful magnifying glass. That dictionary graces the lectern of the library in the Fairy Castle.

Years later, when Ms. Moore was already a famous film star, and her collection of miniatures began to overflow their display cases, her father suggested the idea of building a more elaborate showcase. "This time," he said, "get an architect, engage artists, and build that fairy castle you have always talked about." The results of that effort stand before you.

The castle measures 9 square feet and its highest tower stands 12 feet above the floor. Made of aluminum and constructed in 200 pieces, it contains more than 1,000 miniature treasures collected from around the world. The sides of the castle have been left open, so as you circle the display, you can examine closely the remarkable decor and contents of each "room."

Murals with themes from the great fairy tales of the Brothers Grimm and Hans Christian Andersen adorn the castle walls, which are also hung with tiny portraits and landscaped in ornate gilt frames. The pieces may be miniature, but that doesn't mean they aren't real. The delicate rosewood piano in the drawing room and the stately pipe organ in the chapel actually play music. Each wee book in the library is filled with actual text: there are titles from Sinclair Lewis, F. Scott Fitzgerald, and John Steinbeck, among many others. The many little clocks can tick and chime; the lighting fixtures light and the fountains flow—since the castle is equipped with both an electrical system and running water.

From the sublime, we move on to the macabre. The next exhibit is highly unusual, and as fascinating to many visitors as anything the museum has to offer, the:

9. **U-505 Submarine.** This German "Untersee boot," or U-boat as this submarine class came to be known in English, was captured by the American Navy off the coast of Africa on June 4, 1944. The significance of this capture went way beyond the already considerable act of taking an enemy craft in battle; the sub's capture was a closely guarded secret. Since a critical code book was among the documents captured from the sub, the American Military Command had contrived to convince their German counterparts that U-505 and its entire crew had been lost at sea. The ruse succeeded, and the captured document, which revealed the radio code used by the Germans in directing their U-boat operations, became vital to resupply efforts after the Allies had landed at Normandy, two days after U-505's capture.

Only after the war did the world learn the fate of U-505 and its crew, who sat out the remainder of the conflict in Bermuda. For several months the U-505 made a tour of eastern port cities as a showpiece for a war bond subscription drive, and then it was tied up in the Navy Yard at Portsmouth, New Hampshire, to await final disposition. When Chicago learned of its story and that one of its native sons had been in command at its capture, the Navy was asked if the sub could be brought to the city as a war memorial.

Such a request had to be authorized by Congress, and a considerable war chest of private contributions had to be raised to accomplish this feat. But on June 26, 1954, U-505 finally arrived in Chicago, and was placed on a floating drydock in Lake Michigan only 800 feet from the eastern side of the museum, where the sub would take up its final position as a permanent exhibit. Getting the sub in place was no small task. The U-505 is

253 feet long by 22 feet at its widest point, and about three stories high at the conning tower. Through much creative engineering, the vessel was slid ashore in late August 1954 on a system of rails; a few days later, on a Friday evening, traffic was stopped along the "outer drive" at 7pm, and U-505 was inched across. By 4:15am it had cleared the roadway.

Today you may enter U-505 on a self-guided audiotape tour, and visit the sub's five main compartments. As you can imagine, an enormous amount of equipment is compressed rather ingeniously into a relatively small interior space. The U-505's interior has been compared with the mechanism of a finely tuned watch, and the metaphor is apt, because, like the watch, all the parts and pieces of the submarine had to function with incredible precision. What I found even more bewildering was how a crew of 50 officers and seamen could co-exist and function under such conditions of narrow confinement.

Directly behind the U-505, is an addition to the museum that houses the:

10. Henry Crown Space Center. The Space Center has its own entrance on Columbus Drive, but is also accessible from the ground floor of the museum. Exhibited within this 36,000-square-foot complex are numerous historic artifacts that testify to man's efforts to explore outerspace. Here on display is the Apollo 8 capsule, the first spacecraft to orbit the moon, and an LEM prototype, the Lunar Excursion Module used to train astronauts for Apollo missions. A Mercury spacecraft, the Aurora 7, is also here.

For a more active experience of what space travel actually feels like, take a ride on the full-scale model of a NASA Space Shuttle, containing a 3-D theater simulating lift-off and a space voyage. Those seeking more detailed information on the space program can peruse the "space exploration section," which details some of the program's influences on modern life in the fields of aviation, industry, electronics, and medicine. If you haven't seen one till now, here at the Space Center is also your chance to see a bonafide moonrock.

Also contained within the Henry Crown Space Center is the:

11. Omnimax Theater. As most readers will know, this is a state-of-the-art movie house. The screen, which virtually wraps around the viewing audience, is five stories high and 75 feet in diameter. Whether or not you choose to see the show, which changes about once every six months, you can get some notion of the remarkable technology involved by looking into the projection room, which is fully visible behind a glass partition. The reels for the super 70mm film are gigantic, roughly 10 times the size of normal movie reels; they must be lifted into place mechanically, and then the whole projector raises on its own elevator 18 feet into position in the theater. A special computer regulates the more than half a million commands that can be executed per film showing, and controls as many as 120 slide and special effects projectors. Recent epics have included The Rolling Stones in concert, *Fires of Kuwait*, and *Antarctica*, which was produced and distributed worldwide by the museum.

The final leg of our tour takes us to the Balcony Level, which is accessible by stairs or elevator. The exhibits here are less monumental or technologically dazzling than many of those on the museum's two principal floors. But there is something about the Balcony exhibits reminiscent of the old-fashioned educational mission museums pursued more directly in the past, before they became repositories of corporate propaganda or began competing with theme-park entertainments. The following exhibit, for example, needs no hype or special effects to hold your attention; it is called:

12. Prenatal Development. Originally entitled "Life Before Birth," the specimens on display were first loaned to the museum in 1939 by the Loyola University Medical School. The exhibit demonstrates human embryo and fetus development through a sequence of 40 preserved specimens. The fascination with this eerie display is that all the specimens appear normal, and increasingly so as they progress in developmental stages from conception toward the full term of human gestation. The museum, however, provides a disclaimer to this lay observation, which must be near universal among those who reflect on this lineup of erstwhile babies in jars. In the jargon of a pathologist from a local hospital, whose views have been solicited by the museum, each fetus or embryo you behold as normal is actually "non-viable due to genetic incompatibility." Presumably we can interpret this to mean that the specimens were all abnormal, and were either miscarried or stillborn. What makes this exhibit first rate and educational in the truest sense of the word is that it does not attempt to program one's intellectual or emotional responses, but instead reflects a deep and penetrating reality that provokes genuine wonderment and thought.

Two other very worthwhile exhibits with considerable educational content, displayed over spacious quarters side by side, examine:

13. The Heart and The Brain. Both exhibits serve as introductions to human anatomy and to the function and malfunction of these respective organs. The 16-foot walk-through heart is a bit corny, but an effective visual device, especially for small fry who can more readily distinguish the organ's varied parts when presented on this scale. The brain, of course, is more elusive.

One could look for hours at the many panels depicting the sections and functions of human gray matter on display here and still not have a clue about how the brain functions. And, unlike the heart, which is after all just a fancy pump, the only "brain transplant" ever undertaken was performed by Dr. Frankenstein. Whatever science does know or can speculate about the brain, however, is graphically detailed here in an attractive and straight-forward presentation, which includes a number of hands-on activities.

Our final stop in the museum will be at an exhibit that until the 1990s was virtually unimaginable:

14. **Kids' Starway: A Path to Self Discovery.** No age, and certainly no country, has ever experienced the degree of preoccupation with the "self" as we have witnessed in recent years in the United States. This exhibit, for better or worse—and probably both—is a reflection of that trend. Kids' Starway was developed by a child psychologist especially for children from 7 to 12 years of age and their parents. And once you get beyond the "I'm okay, you're okay" superficiality of most displays, which tend to patronize rather than shed light on human diversity, Kids' Starway performs at least one valuable service. Through a series of interactive displays involving child and parent, the exhibit helps to democratize human emotions across the generations by placing the child's feelings on an equal par with those of the parent.

WALKING TOUR 11

The Loop Sculpture Tour

Start: *Untitled,* by Pablo Picasso, in Richard J. Daley Civic Center Plaza, on Washington Street between Dearborn and Clark streets.
Public Transportation: There's a stop of the Lake/Dan Ryan line at Washington and Dearborn.
Finish: *The Fountain of the Great Lakes,* by Lorado Taft; Michigan Avenue near Jackson Boulevard.
Time: 2 to 3 hours.
Best Times: You can take this tour virtually any time, within reason. Early evening hours after dusk most times of year are not totally out of the question, since the streets are well traveled and well lighted. Some of the sculptures are housed in the lobbies of buildings, and these may be closed after business hours, however. Personal security can be an issue in the Loop after dark, so exercise common sense.

Among all major American cities, Chicago has led the way with its program of public art. Examples of public art—in the form of traditional monuments, murals, and monumental contemporary sculpture—are located widely throughout the city, but their concentration within the Loop and nearby Grant Park has gradually transformed downtown Chicago into a "museum without walls."

Furthermore, while other cities like Portland, Seattle, and Phoenix have also initiated significant public art programs, no municipality even comes close to the scale and importance of the collection in Chicago. In the Loop alone are representative works by many of the most celebrated artists and sculptors of the 20th century.

As in the field of architecture, Chicago public officials and city planners have demonstrated an unusual degree of civic foresight by insisting that growth in the public sphere—in the form of new construction and remodeling of municipal buildings—must include some purely aesthetic contribution. The city's Percent-for-Art ordinance ensures that some percentage of building costs be put aside for artwork. In recent years, many private sector companies have become voluntary partners in this program.

Our tour of this outdoor museum returns us to the Loop, but in this instance our focus will be entirely on the public art, rather than on the world-class architecture covered in Walking Tour 1, "The Loop: Chicago Architecture," and Walking Tour 2, "South Michigan Avenue/Grant Park." Some visitors may wish to combine these tours, or portions thereof, into a single itinerary.

We begin our tour in the Richard J. Daley Civic Center Plaza on Washington Street between Dearborn and Clark streets, before a sculpture whose image has become virtually synonymous with the city of Chicago, called:

1. ***Untitled,* by Pablo Picasso.** The artist donated this design to Chicago when he resolved to not cash the $100,000 check he received from the city. The 50-foot sculpture was executed in Cor-Tan steel at a foundry on the city's south side from a *maquette* provided by Picasso, which is now on display at the Art Institute. *Untitled* was finally installed at Daley Plaza in 1967 to a chorus of public disapproval. Outside a small circle of art sophisticates, the average philistine-in-the-street either hated the work outright or simply confessed to "not understanding" its obscure abstract "message." Clearly, the public had expected more from the great Picasso.

   In time, the sculpture began to grow on people, like some homely mutt at the animal shelter whose profoundly sad eyes make an irrefutable case for instant adoption. As local hearts and minds slowly warmed to *Untitled,* the notion began to circulate that the work's abstraction was indeed based on some model from reality, in fact on two such images: Seen straight on, it was understood to be the likeness of Picasso's favorite hound, Kaboul, and viewed from the side, it would seem to profile a woman.

   With this concrete, if schizophrenic, identity now intact, the sculpture could gradually assume its semi-official status as the logo of modern Chicago. And it is by far the city's most popular photo opportunity among visiting tourists. A delegation of post–Cold War Russian generals recently placed visiting the Picasso as their first priority while touring the sights of the city. No feature film on location in Chicago seems to resist the temptation of working a shot of *Untitled* into its background: witness *The Blues Brothers* and the more recent blockbluster *The Fugitive.*

The wide apron of pavement known as Daley Plaza has itself become a favorite spot for public gatherings, for lunchtime concerts, and for skateboard enthusiasts who execute "rail-slides" on the concrete curb at the base of the sculpture. When Chicagoans want to "tell it to City Hall," which is located in the building across Clark Street, they organize their demonstrations here for that purpose. No public square would be complete without a war memorial: An eternal flame set off to one side of the plaza remembers the veterans of Korea and Vietnam. And finally, presented at noon each weekday is a free cultural series sponsored by the city, featuring music on most occasions, and in season, a Farmer's Market twice a month on Thursdays. Because Picasso gave *Untitled* to the "people of Chicago," no one holds a copyright on the piece; and as you can see, the sculpture is truly within the public domain.

Tucked into a confined plaza across the street next to the Brunswick Building, 69 West Washington Street, is:

2. *Miró's Chicago.* Like the Picasso, Joan Miró's design for this 39-foot statue of steel, wire mesh, concrete, bronze, and ceramic tiles was a gift to the city from the artist, and was likewise executed in Chicago, at a cost of $500,000. The money was raised through a cooperative effort involving the city and a group of private individuals. Miró, however, did have a direct hand in the finished work, having fabricated at his studio in Majorca the ceramic tiles that were pressed into their designated spots soon after the concrete layering was sprayed onto the metal frame.

The statue is supposed to represent a great earth mother, but the reaction of one irate art student after the work's installation was less than maternal, or even fraternal for that matter; he splashed the rounded form with red paint. Most abstract art, of course, is an acquired taste, but this particular Miró creation does look suspiciously like the Pillsbury Doughboy from the neck down. One very nice touch, however, is the bronze plaque with the raised outline of the figure in Braille, allowing the statue to be "seen" by the blind.

Note also the stained-glass window in the building next door.

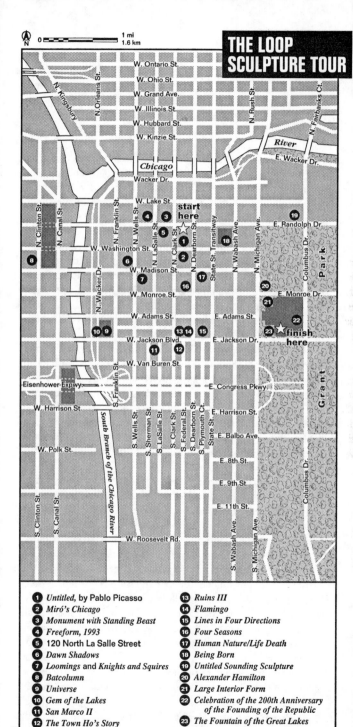

THE LOOP SCULPTURE TOUR

1. *Untitled*, by Pablo Picasso
2. *Miró's Chicago*
3. *Monument with Standing Beast*
4. *Freeform, 1993*
5. 120 North La Salle Street
6. *Dawn Shadows*
7. *Loomings* and *Knights and Squires*
8. *Batcolumn*
9. *Universe*
10. *Gem of the Lakes*
11. *San Marco II*
12. *The Town Ho's Story*
13. *Ruins III*
14. *Flamingo*
15. *Lines in Four Directions*
16. *Four Seasons*
17. *Human Nature/Life Death*
18. *Being Born*
19. *Untitled Sounding Sculpture*
20. *Alexander Hamilton*
21. *Large Interior Form*
22. *Celebration of the 200th Anniversary of the Founding of the Republic*
23. *The Fountain of the Great Lakes*

This is Chicago Temple, at 568 feet the tallest church in the world, according to the *Guinness Book of World Records*. The First Methodist Episcopal Church maintains a sanctuary at street level, and in the spire above the intervening office space, a chapel.

Now walk north one block along Clark Street to the State of Illinois Building on the corner of Randolph Street, where you'll see a work by Jean Dubuffet:

3. *Monument with Standing Beast.* This four-sided enclosure in fiberglass stands 29 feet at its highest point, and may be entered. It represents what Dubuffet described as "drawing which extends . . . into space" to reach the man in the street. Dubuffet is best known for his "art brute," a creative interpretation of the brutality of the urban landscape, incorporating graffiti, street slang, and caricature. This particular work, donated to the city by private foundations, expresses four distinct motifs, none of which are especially harsh or hard-hitting. From one side you see an animal; from another a tree; a third view reveals a portal; and before the fourth wall, you face a Gothic church. "Which," Dubuffet seems to be asking, "is the monument, and which the beast?"

The 17th-story State of Illinois Building, designed by Helmut Jahn, which rises above the Dubuffet, is itself adorned with much artistic jewelry. Nineteen specially commissioned artworks by Illinois artists are scattered throughout the expansive skylit rotunda. Also within the building is a free art gallery run by local artists, where the works displayed are varied, imaginative, and well executed. For one of the great "rides" in the city, cruise the glass-sided elevators, which run up the interior walls of the rotunda, to the 17th floor.

Adorning the exterior facade of the Illinois State Office Building across the street at 160 North La Salle Street is the work of Richard Hunt, called:

4. *Freeform, 1993.* The artist is a native son, trained at the School of the Art Institute, who has achieved international acclaim. This sculpture is typical of his work, which embodies the idea of abstract art as something "freely formed" in the artist's pursuit of a unique form of expression. The stainless-steel figure appears deceptively small, but is actually two-and-a-half-stories high and weighs three tons. The building itself is an instance of an aging structure that was gutted, then completely rejuvenated; the central bay, with its glassed-in court-like lobby is completely new.

Containing two interesting examples of public art is Helmut Jahn's latest building half a block to the south, completed in 1991, at:

5. 120 North La Salle Street. The first is a colorful mosaic by

Roger Brown, which arches above the entrance and is called the *Flight of Daedalus and Icarus.* Inside, at the end of the lobby is the second work, a fascinating and stylized portrayal in relief of Chicago's "Wall Street," called *La Salle Corridor and Holding Pattern,* by John Buck.

Continue walking south and turn right, to the west, on Madison Street. On the corner of Wells is a space called Madison Plaza with a work by the late, incomparable Louise Nevelson:

6. ***Dawn Shadows.*** This expansive 30-foot-high composition in black painted steel, installed in 1983, is said to have been inspired by the superstructure of the elevated train, which runs close to Madison Plaza. The work is very different from the walls of stacked wooden forms and boxes more typically associated with Nevelson. Already near 80 when this public work was commissioned, she no doubt was also influenced considerably by the work of her contemporary, Alexander Calder, and by a younger New York artist whose massive steel structures had achieved such explosive worldwide recognition in the 1970s, Richard Serra. Normally, Nevelson's work demonstrated more originality, a quality that carried over to her dramatic persona. It has always fascinated me that Nevelson and another 20th-century original, Edna St. Vincent Millay, both came from the same sleepy town, Rockland, on the coast of Maine.

On the southeastern corner of Madison Street and Wells is a building called the Paine Webber Tower, at 181 West Madison Street. Adorning the lobby are two companion art pieces by sculptor Frank Stella:

7. ***Loomings*** and ***Knights and Squires.*** The construction firm of Miglin and Beitler, also responsible for the Nevelson sculpture across the street, commissioned these pieces from Frank Stella. Lee Miglin and J. Paul Beitler pride themselves on their commitment to public art, and each of their buildings throughout Chicago is adorned by sculptures commissioned from some well-known 20th-century artist. In planning the building at this particular address, the developers specifically asked architect Cesar Pelli to design the five-story, 100-foot-long marble lobby as a gallery to display Stella's two works.

Frank Stella, whose international reputation began to soar in the late '60s, describes the two pieces as "paintings." In fact, they are low-relief sculptures fabricated from aluminum and magnesium, which were then etched and brightly painted by the artist. The titles of these pieces place the sculptures in Stella's *Moby Dick* series, begun in 1985 when the artist first sought inspiration for his work in Herman Melville's epic story. The two sculptures are quite stunning, and their three-dimensionality invites a close inspection from many angles.

This next work is not conveniently located within the Loop, and can't really be considered a bonafide part of this tour. To see it, you must walk a fair distance east along Madison Street to the fringe of an area called Greek Town. But the sculpture is so unique and zany that it must be mentioned in passing. The true art aficionado may wish to hop a cab from downtown, and just have the driver cruise by Claes Oldenburg's:

8. ***Batcolumn.*** Oldenburg, a native of Sweden who actually grew up in Chicago, was one of the few practitioners of the so-called "Pop Art" in the 1960s who never seemed to take himself too seriously. And yet, the scale of conception of Oldenburg's works, which seem to poke fun at the very essence of American popular culture, elevate his vision to the realm of high art. The *Batcolumn,* located in front of the Social Security Administration Building at 60 West Madison Street, is a prime example of Oldenburg's offbeat whimsy. When first hearing the title of this piece, one imagines it has something to do with Batman, only to discover that Oldenburg's foil is the revered national pastime, baseball. A 100-foot-high Louisville Slugger of latticed Cor-Ten steel, propped up on end upon a stubby cylindrical base is the object that confronts the bewildered viewer.

Whether or not you have treated yourself to this impromptu digression, our tour continues two blocks to the west and south of Madison Plaza, where we enter the lobby of the Sears Tower, 233 South Wacker Drive, to see:

9. ***Universe.*** This is a moving wall sculpture by Alexander Calder, installed here in 1974. We'll have more to say about Calder when we get to one of his more impressive creations, a stabile located further along on this tour (see Stop 14).

While we're in the neighborhood, we'll drop into the Wintergarden, the spectacular entryway to the building next door, 311 South Wacker Drive, to look at a work by architect-turned-sculptor, Raymond Kaskey, called:

10. ***Gem of the Lakes.*** It is the setting of this traditional sculpture, a bronze fountain with classical overtones—in the vast, glass-roofed conservatory attached to this attractive, 65-story postmodern skyscraper—that commands the lion's share of one's appreciation. This public space called the Wintergarden occupies 12,000 square feet under an arched, multipaned glass roof 85 feet high. Two lines of giant palm trees border the pool, which is filled by water flowing from the fountain sculpture; on either side of the palms, two rows of stately columns support the roof and the walls of glass behind them. A French bistro restaurant called Yevette, at the tower end of the Wintergarden, looks very inviting.

Follow Van Buren Street east to the One Financial Place

Plaza at 440 South La Salle Street, where you'll see a bronze horse created by Ludovico de Luigi, called:

11. *San Marco II.* The model for Luigi's bronze was a set of four horses that once graced the facade of St. Mark's Basilica in Venice. Sculpted in Constantinople, the statues had come to Venice as spoils from the Fourth Crusade sometime around the year 1200, where they eventually became decayed and were removed from St. Mark's and placed in storage. As an homage to this "destroyed treasure of his native city," Ludovico de Luigi executed the work seen here. The horse, posed in mid-stride, stands atop a fountain in this public space outside the current headquarters of the Chicago Stock Exchange.

REFUELING STOP It might be interesting to rub elbows with the local traders in one of their favorite watering holes, the **Savoy Bar & Grill** (tel. 663-8800) on the mezzanine level of this same building, 440 South La Salle Street. The Savoy is known for its breakfasts, and a variety of "trader fast foods," as well as cocktails served at off-hours, beginning at 11am.

Walk one block north and east to 77 West Jackson Boulevard, the Ralph H. Metcalfe Federal Building. Here in the lobby is another example of Frank Stella's work, in this instance a monumental sculpture called:

12. *The Town Ho's Story.* Also a part of Stella's *Moby Dick* series, this 18-foot colossus on a 14-foot-wide base is actually a "collage" of several smaller statues, which the artist welded into one large abstract shape. This became a frame over which Stella poured molten aluminum to achieve this final, "enhanced" shape. The sculpture takes its name, *The Town Ho's Story,* according to Melville scholar Robert K. Wallace, "from a chapter of Melville's novel that is a tale about Steelkilt, an audacious sailor who uses both mind and fist to resist mistreatment." The work was commissioned by the federal General Services Administration through its Art-in-Architecture program, and the scale Stella chose for his final design was dictated, in part, by the sheer volume of space in the lobby of the Metcalfe Building.

Directly across the street and outdoors, on the northeast corner of Jackson Boulevard and Clark Street, is a sculpture called:

13. *Ruins III.* An ensemble of forms, the work of sculptor Nita K. Suderland, was installed here in 1978. In many ways, this configuration, while considerably less ambitious, is as appealing

as any of the more grand displays of public art among its contemporary companions within the Loop.

Farther east on Jackson Boulevard, you will come to Federal Center Plaza, which fronts Dearborn Street. Here, stretched across the pavement, stands the vermillion-colored masterpiece of Alexander Calder, called:

14. **Flamingo.** When you see this construction, you might readily imagine that the piece would have been more aptly named *Praying Mantis*. But the images we ascribe to abstract art are no less labile and subjective than the shapes assumed by passing clouds on a lazy summer day. As Calder himself observed, his stabiles have no reference to actual forms. He called his Chicago work *Flamingo* because "it was sort of pink and has a long neck." But somehow, with this single fluid mass of steel rising 53 feet into the air, the artist managed to transform an otherwise sterile plaza into a space more hospitable to the human species. Great numbers traffic this plaza daily. But the workday rush slackens to the pace of a Sunday stroll through an English park when people pass beneath the spreading limbs of Calder's stabile.

Just before you get to State Street, at 10 West Jackson Boulevard, is the work of another minimalist artist, Sol Lewitt, whose success has allowed him to express his ideas on a monumental scale:

15. **Lines in Four Directions.** The work is a 90-by-72-foot relief sculpture nearly eight stories high, installed in 1985 on the brick wall of a small building facing the east facade of the Federal Building. What you see is a screen of white-painted aluminum slats arranged in geometric patterns and projecting two inches from the wall, divided into four equal sections. This "wall project" is a realization in three dimensions of a drawing from a series Lewitt has been working with since 1968.

Return one block west to Dearborn Street, and walk north till Monroe, where in the midst of a recessed space called First National Plaza is the work of Marc Chagall:

16. **Four Seasons.** The work is a rectangular monolith of concrete, sheathed with a mosaic of pastel-colored stone and glass fragments. The six fanciful scenes of Chicago seem to float on the surface of the huge box, 70 feet long, 10 feet wide, and 14 feet high, in that perspectiveless manner that is so characteristic of Chagall. The sculpture was executed in Chicago, but Chagall had worked out the designs at his studio in France, transferring his vision onto full-sized panels, using a palate of 250 different colors. This space around the First National Bank Building is one of the most popular public plazas in downtown Chicago,

THE LOOP SCULPTURE TOUR • 143

CALDER: A PERSONAL RECOLLECTION

Alexander Calder agreed to donate a gouache to a benefit that I was helping to organize in New York City in 1974. I was invited to visit the artist at his home in southern France to discuss the project and to select a canvas for the benefit. Calder lived in the châteaux country, south of Tours, in a little village called Sache. His modern home and studio complex, a series of barnlike structures sheathed in boards, was spread over a very pastoral setting, and managed to blend in amazingly well with the neighboring antiquities.

When I met him, Calder, in his mid-70s, was recovering from a severe stroke and could speak only with great difficulty. But he was a playful man with a great curiosity about the world, and we sat at a trestle table, facing each other across a good bottle of French claret. Calder listened intently as I made my pitch to his American expatriate son-in-law. Calder then motioned me to another table, where he personally conducted a tour, mostly in mime, of his wonderful circus of tiny animals and apparatus made from wire and string. Then we went for a stroll on the grounds behind the studio, and walked among the dozen or so completed stabiles and mobiles towering above us, waiting there to be shipped to destinations around the world. It was an exhilarating moment, and I confess to feeling awed as much by the man himself, with his warm and unassuming manner, as I was by the near overdose of exposure to that powerful garden of giant sculptures. We returned to the house, taking up our positions again at the table, and Calder reached for another bottle of Bordeaux. His formidable wife, Luisa, who had till that moment remained in the background, now intervened pointedly, saying, "Sandy, don't use this visit as an excuse to get drunk." To which Calder, in the clearest words he was to speak that day, replied, "Don't need no excuse."

especially at lunchtime and in the hours immediately following the workday during warm weather.

One of the more unconventional pieces of public art to be found in the Loop is this next work by Bruce Nauman, on the State Street Mall, near the corner of Madison Street, called:

17. *Human Nature/Life Death.* Nauman based the idea for this neon sculpture on those flashing neon beer signs you see in bars and bodegas all over the country. He decided to employ this medium to get his own message across. Your first reaction when you see the piece is that it's just another advertising sign, until you read what it says. Then, the artist says, "you have to think about it." The message here on this six-foot circular sculpture is conveyed with four pairs of words, life/death, love/hate, pleasure/pain, and human nature/animal nature, which flash independently in a pattern that repeats every few minutes.

Don't neglect to take in the ornamental facade of the Carson Pirie Scott Department, the work of Louis Sullivan, on the southeast corner of State and Madison Streets. This work is discussed more fully in Walking Tour 1, "The Loop: Chicago Architecture," but it never suffers from overexposure.

Another block north along the State Street Mall, at the northeast corner with Washington Street, will bring you to a work by Virginio Ferrari, called:

18. *Being Born.* This sculpture pays homage to the tool-and-die industry, which commissioned and fabricated the work. Two stainless-steel circles, the larger of which is nearly 20 feet in diameter, fit exactly into each other to symbolize the process of die making. The sculpture is supported by a round granite base whose central surface is covered with water and serves as a reflecting pool. For Ferarri, who was born in Verona to a family of stonecutters and was at one time an artist in residence at the University of Chicago, this interest in geometric precision is typical of his work in recent years.

Now proceed north one block, cross Michigan Avenue and walk to 200 East Randolph Street, where in the Amoco Building Plaza, adjoining the second tallest building in the world, is an environmental sculpture designed by Harry Bertoia, called:

19. *Untitled Sounding Sculpture.* The units of thin copper rods, standing upright in a large reflecting pool, are activated by the wind and vibrate at different frequencies, producing pleasing musical tones. Bertoia's image for this work recalls fields of wheat blowing in the wind, combined with the mythological notion of the Aeolian harp. The artist came to the United States from Italy at the age of 15 and ultimately studied architecture under the Finnish master, Eliel Saarinen. Harry Bertoia is best known for the celebrated wire chair he designed in 1952.

Return now to Michigan Avenue, and walk south. Between Madison and Monroe streets, on the park side of the avenue, is a monument you might wish to look at in passing, the statue of:

20. *Alexander Hamilton.* This over-lifesize figure of Hamilton was installed in 1918, during the period when Grant Park was being formally laid out. The sculptor, Bela Lyon Pratt, had studied with Augustus Saint-Gaudens, and this work, cast posthumously, was his last. The statue memorializes the long-standing American romance with Hamilton, a quintessential role model of modern capitalism.

Across Monroe Street, in a space called the Stanley McCormick Memorial Court, is a tall bronze sculpture designed by Henry Moore, called:

21. *Large Interior Form.* This work, installed in 1983, is a separate cast of the "inner element" of a larger construction in the lobby of Three First National Plaza, called *Large Upright Internal/External Form.* Both works explore the sensuality inherent in natural forms, an infatuation at the core of Moore's lifelong curiosity to understand "what three-dimensionality is all about."

Moore was the son of a Yorkshire coalminer who won a scholarship to study at London's Royal College of Art. Moore suggests that much of the inspiration for his work came from the collections of primitive non-Western sculpture in the British Museum, which the young art student visited often in his spare time. Moore preferred to create sculptures for the outdoors. There are four additional examples of Moore's work, placed in natural settings, throughout Chicago and its environs: *Nuclear Energy* and *Reclining Figure* at the University of Chicago, *Sundial* at the Adler Planetarium, and *Large Two Forms* at the Gould Center in Rolling Meadows.

Another world-class name in sculpture, Isamu Noguchi, is represented in Chicago with his work in Grant Park, on the east facade of the Art Institute complex at Columbus Drive between Monroe Street and Jackson Boulevard. The work goes by the long name of:

22. *Celebration of the 200th Anniversary of the Founding of the Republic.* The California-born Noguchi's work was installed here in 1976 to commemorate the American Bicentennial. The highly stylized fountain "integrates the visual poetry of a Japanese garden with the precision of modern technology." The entire work is shaped from three-million-year-old rainbow granite quarried in nearby Minnesota. Other than the pool itself, the two principal elements of this construction are an upright, L-shaped pillar, and a low horizontal cylinder, split down the middle; both are vehicles for water, which flows into the surrounding basin. The first form represents a tree, the second a natural spring.

No tour of Chicago's public art would be complete without acknowledging the Illinois native, Lorado Taft, whose works adorn the city of Chicago in many quarters. This tour will end on Michigan Avenue near Jackson Boulevard, with this example of Taft's exceptional talent:

23. ***The Fountain of the Great Lakes.*** Taft credits his inspiration for this work to a remark by architect Daniel H. Burnham, that no one had ever personified the Great Lakes in a work of art. When Taft received a commission by the Art Institute to create a public fountain, he also accepted Burnham's challenge, and chose a classical theme to carry it out. The mythological story of the Danaides, 49 beautiful sisters who were doomed for eternity to carry water in sieves, suggested to Taft the idea of five classical female figures carrying conch shells, and positioned in such a way that water flows from one shell to another. In the sculptor's words, "'Superior' on high, and 'Michigan' on the side both empty into the basin of 'Huron' who sends the stream to 'Erie' whence 'Ontario' receives it . . ." Taft, who grew up in Elmwood, Illinois, is another example of a local talent who first made his mark internationally at the 1893 World's Columbian Fair.

Essentials

The real spice of Chicago can only be savored by walking its streets. You cannot truly claim to have gotten to know a city that you haven't crisscrossed by foot. Chicago is fertile ground for long excursions. Skyscrapers give way to green spaces, which in turn yield to industrial wastelands and riverscapes (the Chicago River seems to be everywhere). Let this guide be your introduction to discovering Chicago by foot. Obviously, you can't wander off just everywhere. Use your own instincts coupled with local information from your hotel staff and the tourist office to set realistic boundaries.

ORIENTATION/CITY LAYOUT

Chicago's streets are laid out in a grid system. From this original rectangular overlay, the city's actual, somewhat stubby and elongated dimensions seem to have been cut out haphazardly. The resulting shape may be irregular, but the graphic pattern remains, and the streets continue to run true, up and down, side to side. The great exceptions are the city's half dozen or so major diagonal thoroughfares, which are said to follow old Native American trails, and, of course, the interconnected network of freeways.

Street numbering, moreover, does not originate at the city's

N

Lake Michigan

N. Lake Shore Dr.

Lincoln Park

Chicago River

geographical midpoint, but nearer to Chicago's historic and commercial center, more north than south, and so far east as almost to border Lake Michigan.

FINDING AN ADDRESS Point zero is located at the downtown intersection of State and Madison streets; State divides east and west addresses and Madison divides north and south addresses. From

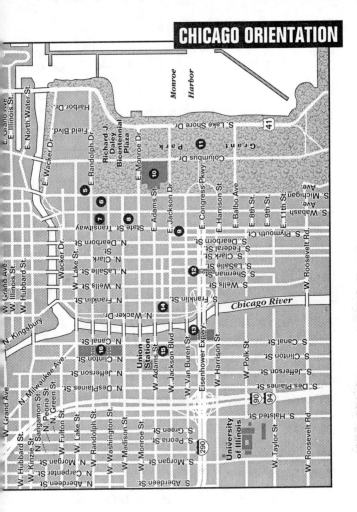

6959

here, Chicago's highly predictable addressing system begins. Making use of this grid, it is relatively easy to plot the distance in miles between any two points in the city.

Virtually all of Chicago's principal north-south and east-west arteries are spaced by increments of 400 in the addressing system—regardless of the number of smaller streets nestled between them. And each addition or subtraction of 400 numbers to an address is equivalent to half a mile. Thus, starting at point zero on Madison Street, and traveling north along State Street for one mile, you will come to 800 North State Street, which intersects Chicago Avenue. Continue uptown for another half mile and you arrive at the 1200 block of North State Street at Division Street. And so it goes right to the city line, with suburban Evanston located at the 7600 block north, 9½ miles from this arbitrary center.

The same rule applies when traveling south or east to west. Thus, heading west from State Street along Madison, Halsted Street—at 800 West Madison Street—is a mile's distance, while Racine, at the 1200 block of West Madison, is 1½ miles from the center. Madison then continues westward to Chicago's boundary along Austin Avenue with the near suburb of Oak Park, which at 6000 West Madison Street is approximately 7½ miles from point zero.

The key to understanding the grid is that the side of any square formed by the principal avenues (noted in dark or red ink on most maps) represents a distance of half a mile in any direction. Understanding how Chicago's grid system works is of particular importance to those visitors who wish to walk a lot in the city's many neighborhoods, and who want to plot in advance the distances involved in trekking from one locale to another.

GETTING AROUND

BY PUBLIC TRANSPORTATION

The Chicago Transit Authority (CTA) operates an extensive system of trains and buses throughout the city of Chicago. The sturdy system carries more than two million passengers a day. Subways and elevated trains are generally safe and reliable, though it's advisable to avoid long rides through unfamiliar neighborhoods late at night.

The METRA commuter railroads and PACE buses operate between the city and surrounding suburbs.

CTA INFORMATION The CTA operates a useful telephone information service (tel. 836-7000 that functions daily from 4:45am to 1am. When you wish to know how to get from where you are to where you want to go, call the CTA. Make sure you specify any conditions you might require—the fastest route, for example, or the simplest (the route with the fewest transfers or least amount of walking), and so forth.

An excellent CTA map is available at subway or El fare booths, or by calling 836-7000.

BY THE EL AND THE SUBWAY The Rapid Transit system operates four major lines, north/south, west/south, west/northwest

CHICAGO TRANSIT SYSTEM

Lake Street/ Dan Ryan Route

LAKE STREET

- 🚈 Harlem
- 🚈 Oak Park
- 🚈 Ridgeland
- 🚈 Austin
- 🚈 Central
- 🚈 Laramie
- 🚈 Cicero
- 🚈 Pulaski
- 🅱 Homan
- 🅐 Kedzie
- 🅐 Ashland
- 🅱 Halsted
- 🚈 Clinton
- (see Downtown Stations map)
- 🅱 Cermak/Chinatown
- 🚈 Sox/35th St.
- 🅐 47th St.
- 🅱 Garfield
- 🅐 63rd St.
- 🚈 69th St.
- 🚈 79th St.
- 🚈 87th St.
- 🚈 95th St.

DAN RYAN

O'Hare/Congress/ Douglas Route

O'HARE

- 🚈 O'Hare
- 🚈 River Road
- 🚈 Cumberland
- 🚈 Harlem
- 🚈 Jefferson Park
- 🅐 Montrose
- 🅐 Irving Park
- 🅱 Addison
- 🚈 Belmont
- 🚈 Logan Square
- 🅐 California
- 🅱 Western
- 🚈 Damen
- 🅐 Division
- 🚈 Chicago
- 🅱 Grand
- (see Downtown Stations map)
- 🚈 Clinton
- 🚈 Halsted/U of I
- 🚈 Racine

LEGEND:
- 🅐 A Train stop
- 🅱 B Train stop
- 🚈 A & B Trains stop

Polk 🅱   18th St. 🅱

CONGRESS

- 🅐 Medical Center
- 🅐 Western
- 🅐 Kedzie/Homan
- 🅐 Pulaski
- 🅐 Cicero
- 🅐 Austin
- 🅐 Oak Park
- 🅐 Harlem
- 🅐 DesPlaines

DOUGLAS

- 🅱 Hoyne
- 🅱 Western
- 🅱 California
- 🅱 Kedzie
- 🅱 Central Park
- 🅱 Pulaski
- 🅱 Kildare
- 🅱 Cicero
- 🅱 54/Cermak

6570A

(the O'Hare train), and a zig-zag northern route called the Ravenswood line. A separate express line services Evanston, while a smaller, local line in Skokie is linked to the north/south train. Skokie and Evanston are adjacent suburbs on Chicago's northern boundary.

Study your CTA map carefully before boarding any train. During the working day (6am to 7pm), A and B trains on all lines make

To EVANSTON

Howard/Englewood/Jackson Park Route

To SKOKIE

	Station
AB	HOWARD
A	Jarvis
AB	Morse
A	Loyola
B	Granville
A	Thorndale
AB	Bryn Mawr
B	Berwyn
A	Argyle
B	Lawrence
AB	Wilson
A	Sheridan
B	Addison
AB	Belmont
AB	Fullerton
A	North/Clybourn
AB	Clark/Division
AB	Chicago
AB	Grand
	(see Downtown Stations map)
AB	Roosevelt
AB	Tech/35th St.
A	Indiana
AB	43rd St.
AB	47th St.
AB	51st St.
AB	Garfield
A	58th St.

To ENGLEWOOD

To JACKSON PARK

LEGEND:
- **A** — A Train stop
- **B** — B Train stop
- **AB** — A & B Trains stop

Ravenswood Route

	Station
AB	Kimball
AB	Kedzie
A	Francisco
B	Rockwell
AB	Western
A	Damen
B	Montrose
AB	Irving Park
A	Addison
A	Paulina
B	Southport
AB	Belmont
A	Wellington
AB	Diversey
AB	Fullerton
AB	Armitage
B	Sedgwick
AB	Chicago
	(see Downtown Stations map)

65708

alternate stops. However, major stations, including all downtown stations (except State/Harrison), are combined A-B stops throughout the day. While most trains run around the clock, decreasing in frequency in the off-peak and overnight hours, some stations close after work hours (as early as 8:30pm) and remain closed on Saturday, Sunday, and holidays. Other stops will remain open on weekends and holidays despite the fact that their fare booths are closed. Simply

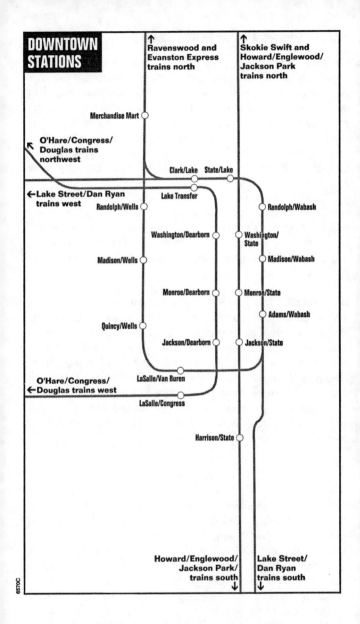

DOWNTOWN STATIONS

Ravenswood and Evanston Express trains north ↑

Skokie Swift and Howard/Englewood/ Jackson Park trains north ↑

Merchandise Mart

O'Hare/Congress/ Douglas trains northwest ↖

Clark/Lake   State/Lake

←Lake Street/Dan Ryan trains west

Lake Transfer

Randolph/Wells   Randolph/Wabash

Washington/Dearborn   Washington/ State

Madison/Wells   Madison/Wabash

Monroe/Dearborn   Monroe/State

Adams/Wabash

Quincy/Wells

Jackson/Dearborn   Jackson/State

LaSalle/Van Buren

O'Hare/Congress/ ←Douglas trains west

LaSalle/Congress

Harrison/State

Howard/Englewood/ Jackson Park/ trains south ↓

Lake Street/ Dan Ryan trains south ↓

6570C

climb to the platform and board the train; a conductor will collect your fare and provide necessary transfers on the train itself. A special Sunday/holiday supertransfer is available that entitles you to unlimited riding (including return trip) from 3am on Sunday (or holiday) mornings to 3am the following day. Under normal circumstances, however, you may not use your transfer on the line where you first obtained it.

BY BUS   Add to Chicago's grid-like layout a comprehensive system of public buses and there is virtually no place in the city that you can't get to that isn't within a short walk from a bus stop. Truly, other than on foot, the best way to get around Chicago's warren of neighborhoods, the best way to actually see what's around you, is while riding a public bus. (The view from the elevated trains can be pretty dramatic, too. The difference is that on the trains you get the backyards, while on the bus you see the buildings' facades and the streetlife.)

PACE buses (tel. toll free 800/972-7000) service the suburban zones that surround Chicago. They run every 20 to 30 minutes during rush hour, operating until mid-evening Monday through Friday, and early evening on weekends. Suburban bus routes are marked 208 and above, and vehicles may be flagged down at intersections since few of the lines have bus stops that are marked.

BY TRAIN   The METRA commuter railroad (tel. 836-7000), which services the suburban zones that surround Chicago, has terminals at several downtown locations, including Union Station at Adams and Canal, La Salle Street Station at La Salle and Van Buren, Northwestern Station at Madison and Canal, and Randolph Street Station at Randolph and Michigan Avenue. The Illinois Central-Gulf Railroad, known locally as the IC, runs close to Lake Michigan on tracks that occupy some of the most valuable real estate in Chicago, and will take you to Hyde Park. Commuter trains have graduated fare schedules based on the distance you ride.

BY TAXI

Taxis are very affordable for getting around Chicago on short runs—for moving around the downtown area, for example, or for excursions to Near North Side neighborhoods of Old Town or Lincoln Park or to Wicker Park on the Near West Side. Beyond that, as in any large city, a cab ride is not economical. Even budget travelers, or those not blessed with generous expense accounts, will find taxis a viable transportation option for the short runs, however.

Some cab companies are American (tel. 248-7600), Yellow/Checker (tel. 829-4222), and Flash (tel. 561-1444).

BY CAR

Chicago is spread out so logically (with each individual area retaining its unbroken connection to the whole) that even for a stranger, driving around the city is a relatively easy task. Rush-hour traffic jams, however, are as daunting in Chicago as in other U.S. cities. On the whole, traffic seems to run fairly smoothly at most times of the day. The combination of wide streets and strategically spaced expressways running in all directions makes for generally easy riding.

The great diagonal corridors violate the grid pattern at key points in the city, and shorten many a trip that would otherwise be tedious on the checkerboard surface of the Chicago streets. Lake Shore Drive (also known as the Outer Drive) has to be one of the most scenic and useful urban thoroughfares to be found anywhere. You can travel the length of the city (and beyond) never far from the great sea-lake that is certainly Chicago's most awesome natural feature.

RENTALS There are outlets of the "big four" car-rental companies in Chicago: Avis (tel. 694-5600), Budget (tel. 686-4950), Hertz (tel. 686-7272), and National (tel. 694-4640).

DRIVING RULES One bizarre anomaly in the organization of Chicago's traffic is the absence of signal lights off the principal avenues. Thus, a block east or west of the Magnificent Mile (North Michigan Avenue)—one of the most traveled streets in the city—you will only encounter stop signs to control the flow of traffic. Once you've become accustomed to the system, it works very smoothly, with everyone—pedestrians and motorists alike—advancing in their proper turn. A right turn on red is allowed unless otherwise posted.

PARKING Parking regulations are vigorously enforced throughout the city of Chicago. There are few urban experiences more discouraging than having to retrieve your impounded car from the police tow-away lot. To avoid unpleasantness, be sure to check parking signs at curbside, and if you run out of luck, find a parking lot and pay the premium prices as you would in any metropolitan area.

Public parking lots are available at the following locations: Grant Park Parking, Michigan Avenue at Congress, and Michigan Avenue at Monroe (tel. 294-2437); MAP Parking, 350 North Orleans (tel. 986-6822); McCormick Place Parking, 2301 South Lake Shore Drive (tel. 294-4600); Midcontinental Plaza Garage, 55 East Monroe (tel. 986-6821); and Navy Pier Parking, 601 East Grand (tel. 791-7437).

BY BOAT

A shuttle boat operates from April through October between a dock adjacent to the Michigan Avenue Bridge and Northwestern Station, a suburban train station across the river from downtown. The ride each way takes about 10 minutes, and is popular with both visitors and commuters. The service operates in the morning from

7:45 to 8:45am from the station, and in the afternoon from 4:45 to 5:27pm from the bridge.

FAST FACTS: CHICAGO

American Express   Travel service offices are located at the following locations: 34 North Clark (tel. 263-6617); 122 South Michigan Avenue (tel. 435-2595); 230 S. Clark (tel. 629-0685); and 625 North Michigan Avenue (tel. 435-2570). All are open Monday through Friday from 9am to 5pm, and the office at 625 North Michigan Avenue is also open on Saturday from 10am to 3pm.

Area Code   Area codes for Chicago and vicinity are 312 and 708.

Bookstores   The big chain bookstores, for the most part, are found in the large suburban shopping malls outside the city. In town, there are many excellent smaller shops, like Barbara's Bookstore in Old Town at 1350 North Wells Street (tel. 642-5044); Stuart Brent Books on the Magnificent Mile at 670 North Michigan Avenue (tel. 337-6357); O'Gara and Wilson in Hyde Park at 1311 East 57th Street (tel. 363-0993).

Business Hours   Shops generally keep normal business hours, opening around 9am and closing by 6pm Monday through Saturday. These days, however, most stores generally stay open late at least one evening a week. And certain businesses, like bookstores, are almost always open during the evening hours all week long. More and more shops are now open on Sunday as well, usually for a half day, during the afternoon. Malls, like Water Tower Place at 835 North Michigan Avenue, are generally open until 8pm, and are open Sunday as well.

Banking hours in Chicago are normally from 9am (8am in some cases) to 3pm Monday through Friday, with select banks remaining open later on specified afternoons and evenings.

Climate   Chicago has a four-season climate, with extremes of cold and heat at both ends. The average temperature in January, generally the coldest month, is 25°F (−4°C); in July and August, the hottest months, the average temperature is 75°F (24°C).

Emergencies   The city of Chicago proclaims the following policy: "In emergency dial 911 and a city ambulance will respond free of charge to the patient. The ambulance will take the patient to the nearest emergency room according to geographic location." If you desire a specific, non-public ambulance, call the Ambulance Service Corporation (tel. 248-2712).

Libraries   The new and exquisite Harold Washington Library

Center is an extremely well-stocked repository of the printed word, located at 400 North State Street (tel. 747-4300).

Lost Property   There is a lost-and-found service at O'Hare International Airport (tel. 686-2201).

Newspapers/Magazines   The *Chicago Tribune* and the *Chicago Sun-Times* are the two major dailies. The *Chicago Reader* is an excellent weekly, distributed free with excellent articles of local interest and all current entertainment and restaurant listings.

Restrooms   Fast-food outlets like McDonald's or Burger King, at various locations around the city, are always a good bet for clean restrooms, as are the lobbies of hotels.

Safety   Whenever you're traveling in an unfamiliar city or country, stay alert. Be aware of your immediate surroundings. Wear a moneybelt and don't sling your camera or purse over your shoulder. This will minimize the possibility of your becoming a victim of crime. Every society has its criminals. It's your responsibility to be aware and be alert even in the most heavily touristed areas.

In Chicago be careful of where you walk alone at night. Consult your hotel concierge or personnel or a local resident if in doubt.

Taxes   The local sales tax is 8.75%. Be sure to calculate the tax when you are budgeting for accommodations and meals.

Tourist Information   The Chicago Office of Tourism can be reached at 744-2400 (toll-free tel. 800/487-2446). There are visitor information booths at the Chicago Cultural Center (78 E. Washington St.) and at the Historic Water Tower (806 N. Michigan Ave.); both are open weekdays 10am to 6pm, Saturday 10am to 5pm, and Sunday noon to 5pm.

Useful Telephone Numbers   For directory assistance, dial 411; for the time, dial 976-1616. For the weather forecast, dial 976-1212.

RECOMMENDED READING

NON-FICTION   For the reader who wishes to delve more deeply into Chicago history, or to study the lives of the city's great builders, the following titles provide a point of departure.

William J. Adelman, a labor historian at the University of Illinois, has written two important works about the labor battles that dominated Chicago's civic and economic life in the late nineteenth century: *Haymarket Revisited* (1986) and *Touring Pullman* (1977), both published by the Illinois Labor History Society. Ross Miller has written a revisionist account of Chicago's development, *American Apocalypse: The Great Fire and the Myth of Chicago* (University of Chicago, 1990).

Dozens of titles document the life and work of Frank Lloyd Wright. Rizzoli has recently published the richly illustrated *Frank Lloyd Wright: The Masterworks* (1993), with text written by Bruce Brooks Pfeiffer. There is John Zukowsky's *Chicago Architecture 1872–1922: Birth of a Metropolis* (Prestel Verlag, 1987) for background on the growth of the Chicago School. *The Architecture of John Wellborn Root* (Johns Hopkins, 1973), by Donald Hoffmann, is an authoritative assessment of that architect. For a definitive biography of another Chicago master, read Hugh Morrison's *Louis Sullivan, Prophet of Modern Architecture* (Peter Smith, 1958).

FICTION So many great American writers have either come from Chicago, lived here during their productive years, or set their work within the city's confines, that it would be impossible to recommend a single book that captures Chicago in its essence. Each of these literary chroniclers provides an intriguing detail of the whole, a captivating aspect of the city that rings true, without pretending to provide the entire melody of the place.

James T. Farrell's trilogy *Studs Lonigan,* published in the thirties, would be one place to start if you want to understand the power of ethnic and neighborhood identity in Chicago. Certain works of novelists Theodore Dreiser *(Sister Carrie)* and Upton Sinclair *(The Jungle),* and of journalist, sports columnist, and short-story writer Ring Lardner, all apply.

Other books set (in full or in part) within the city are Clancy Sigal's *Going Away,* John Dos Passos's *USA Trilogy,* Philip Roth's *Letting Go,* and Saul Bellow's *The Adventures of Augie March* and *Humboldt's Gift.* Richard Wright spent time in Chicago and wrote about it in *Native Son* and *Cooley High.* Hemingway was a native son (Oak Park), though he didn't write much about the city. Chicago has had several fabled poets, including Carl Sandburg and Vachel Lindsay, and the brilliant troubador and popular novelist Nelson Algren *(The Man with the Golden Arm; Walk on the Wild Side),* whose prose-poem *Chicago: City on the Make* is a work of literary beauty. Even Bertolt Brecht set a play, *Saint Joan of the Stockyards,* in Chicago.

And, of course, no one has given a voice to the people of Chicago as has Studs Terkel—in *Division Street America, Hard Times,* and *Working.* These books as well as his own paean to the city, *Chicago,* reveal much about the city he adopted as his own.

Index

Please Send Me the Books Checked Below:

FROMMER'S COMPREHENSIVE GUIDES
(Guides listing facilities from budget to deluxe,
with emphasis on the medium-priced)

	Retail Price	Code		Retail Price	Code
☐ Acapulco/Ixtapa/Taxco 1993–94	$15.00	C120	☐ Morocco 1992–93	$18.00	C021
☐ Alaska 1994–95	$17.00	C131	☐ Nepal 1994–95	$18.00	C126
☐ Arizona 1993–94	$18.00	C101	☐ New England 1994 (Avail. 1/94)	$16.00	C137
☐ Australia 1992–93	$18.00	C002	☐ New Mexico 1993–94	$15.00	C117
☐ Austria 1993–94	$19.00	C119	☐ New York State 1994–95	$19.00	C133
☐ Bahamas 1994–95	$17.00	C121	☐ Northwest 1994–95 (Avail. 2/94)	$17.00	C140
☐ Belgium/Holland/ Luxembourg 1993–94	$18.00	C106	☐ Portugal 1994–95 (Avail. 2/94)	$17.00	C141
☐ Bermuda 1994–95	$15.00	C122	☐ Puerto Rico 1993–94	$15.00	C103
☐ Brazil 1993–94	$20.00	C111	☐ Puerto Vallarta/ Manzanillo/Guadalajara 1994–95 (Avail. 1/94)	$14.00	C028
☐ California 1994	$15.00	C134	☐ Scandinavia 1993–94	$19.00	C135
☐ Canada 1994–95 (Avail. 4/94)	$19.00	C145	☐ Scotland 1994–95 (Avail. 4/94)	$17.00	C146
☐ Caribbean 1994	$18.00	C123	☐ South Pacific 1994–95 (Avail. 1/94)	$20.00	C138
☐ Carolinas/Georgia 1994–95	$17.00	C128	☐ Spain 1993–94	$19.00	C115
☐ Colorado 1994–95 (Avail. 3/94)	$16.00	C143	☐ Switzerland/ Liechtenstein 1994–95 (Avail. 1/94)	$19.00	C139
☐ Cruises 1993–94	$19.00	C107	☐ Thailand 1992–93	$20.00	C033
☐ Delaware/Maryland 1994–95 (Avail. 1/94)	$15.00	C136	☐ U.S.A. 1993–94	$19.00	C116
☐ England 1994	$18.00	C129	☐ Virgin Islands 1994–95	$13.00	C127
☐ Florida 1994	$18.00	C124	☐ Virginia 1994–95 (Avail. 2/94)	$14.00	C142
☐ France 1994–95	$20.00	C132	☐ Yucatán 1993–94	$18.00	C110
☐ Germany 1994	$19.00	C125			
☐ Italy 1994	$19.00	C130			
☐ Jamaica/Barbados 1993–94	$15.00	C105			
☐ Japan 1994–95 (Avail. 3/94)	$19.00	C144			

FROMMER'S $-A-DAY GUIDES
(Guides to low-cost tourist accommodations and facilities)

	Retail Price	Code		Retail Price	Code
☐ Australia on $45 1993–94	$18.00	D102	☐ Israel on $45 1993–94	$18.00	D101
☐ Costa Rica/Guatemala/ Belize on $35 1993–94	$17.00	D108	☐ Mexico on $45 1994	$19.00	D116
☐ Eastern Europe on $30 1993–94	$18.00	D110	☐ New York on $70 1994–95	$16.00	D120
☐ England on $60 1994	$18.00	D112	☐ New Zealand on $45 1993–94	$18.00	D103
☐ Europe on $50 1994	$19.00	D115	☐ Scotland/Wales on $50 1992–93	$18.00	D019
☐ Greece on $45 1993–94	$19.00	D100	☐ South America on $40 1993–94	$19.00	D109
☐ Hawaii on $75 1994	$19.00	D113	☐ Turkey on $40 1992–93	$22.00	D023
☐ India on $40 1992–93	$20.00	D010	☐ Washington, D.C. on $40 1994–95 (Avail. 2/94)	$17.00	D119
☐ Ireland on $45 1994–95 (Avail. 1/94)	$17.00	D117			

FROMMER'S CITY $-A-DAY GUIDES
(Pocket-size guides to low-cost tourist accommodations and facilities)

	Retail Price	Code		Retail Price	Code
☐ Berlin on $40 1994–95	$12.00	D111	☐ Madrid on $50 1994–95 (Avail. 1/94)	$13.00	D118
☐ Copenhagen on $50 1992–93	$12.00	D003	☐ Paris on $50 1994–95	$12.00	D117
☐ London on $45 1994–95	$12.00	D114	☐ Stockholm on $50 1992–93	$13.00	D022

FROMMER'S WALKING TOURS
(With routes and detailed maps, these companion guides point out the places and pleasures that make a city unique)

	Retail Price	Code		Retail Price	Code
☐ Berlin	$12.00	W100	☐ Paris	$12.00	W103
☐ London	$12.00	W101	☐ San Francisco	$12.00	W104
☐ New York	$12.00	W102	☐ Washington, D.C.	$12.00	W105

FROMMER'S TOURING GUIDES
(Color-illustrated guides that include walking tours, cultural and historic sights, and practical information)

	Retail Price	Code		Retail Price	Code
☐ Amsterdam	$11.00	T001	☐ New York	$11.00	T008
☐ Barcelona	$14.00	T015	☐ Rome	$11.00	T010
☐ Brazil	$11.00	T003	☐ Scotland	$10.00	T011
☐ Florence	$ 9.00	T005	☐ Sicily	$15.00	T017
☐ Hong Kong/Singapore/ Macau	$11.00	T006	☐ Tokyo	$15.00	T016
☐ Kenya	$14.00	T018	☐ Turkey	$11.00	T013
☐ London	$13.00	T007	☐ Venice	$ 9.00	T014

FROMMER'S FAMILY GUIDES

	Retail Price	Code		Retail Price	Code
☐ California with Kids	$18.00	F100	☐ San Francisco with Kids (Avail. 4/94)	$17.00	F104
☐ Los Angeles with Kids (Avail. 4/94)	$17.00	F103	☐ Washington, D.C. with Kids (Avail. 2/94)	$17.00	F102
☐ New York City with Kids (Avail. 2/94)	$18.00	F101			

FROMMER'S CITY GUIDES
(Pocket-size guides to sightseeing and tourist accommodations and facilities in all price ranges)

	Retail Price	Code		Retail Price	Code
☐ Amsterdam 1993–94	$13.00	S110	☐ Montréal/Québec City 1993–94	$13.00	S125
☐ Athens 1993–94	$13.00	S114	☐ Nashville/Memphis 1994–95 (Avail. 4/94)	$13.00	S141
☐ Atlanta 1993–94	$13.00	S112	☐ New Orleans 1993–94	$13.00	S103
☐ Atlantic City/Cape May 1993–94	$13.00	S130	☐ New York 1994 (Avail. 1/94)	$13.00	S138
☐ Bangkok 1992–93	$13.00	S005	☐ Orlando 1994	$13.00	S135
☐ Barcelona/Majorca/ Minorca/Ibiza 1993–94	$13.00	S115	☐ Paris 1993–94	$13.00	S109
☐ Berlin 1993–94	$13.00	S116	☐ Philadelphia 1993–94	$13.00	S113
☐ Boston 1993–94	$13.00	S117	☐ San Diego 1993–94	$13.00	S107
☐ Budapest 1994–95 (Avail. 2/94)	$13.00	S139	☐ San Francisco 1994	$13.00	S133
☐ Chicago 1993–94	$13.00	S122	☐ Santa Fe/Taos/ Albuquerque 1993–94	$13.00	S108
☐ Denver/Boulder/ Colorado Springs 1993–94	$13.00	S131	☐ Seattle/Portland 1994–95	$13.00	S137
☐ Dublin 1993–94	$13.00	S128	☐ St. Louis/Kansas City 1993–94	$13.00	S127
☐ Hong Kong 1994–95 (Avail. 4/94)	$13.00	S140	☐ Sydney 1993–94	$13.00	S129
☐ Honolulu/Oahu 1994	$13.00	S134	☐ Tampa/St. Petersburg 1993–94	$13.00	S105
☐ Las Vegas 1993–94	$13.00	S121	☐ Tokyo 1992–93	$13.00	S039
☐ London 1994	$13.00	S132	☐ Toronto 1993–94	$13.00	S126
☐ Los Angeles 1993–94	$13.00	S123	☐ Vancouver/Victoria 1994–95 (Avail. 1/94)	$13.00	S142
☐ Madrid/Costa del Sol 1993–94	$13.00	S124	☐ Washington, D.C. 1994 (Avail. 1/94)	$13.00	S136
☐ Miami 1993–94	$13.00	S118			
☐ Minneapolis/St. Paul 1993–94	$13.00	S119			

SPECIAL EDITIONS

	Retail Price	Code		Retail Price	Code
☐ Bed & Breakfast Southwest	$16.00	P100	☐ Caribbean Hideaways	$16.00	P103
☐ Bed & Breakfast Great American Cities (Avail. 1/94)	$16.00	P104	☐ National Park Guide 1994 (Avail. 3/94)	$16.00	P105
			☐ Where to Stay U.S.A.	$15.00	P102

Please note: if the availability of a book is several months away, we may have back issues of guides to that particular destination. Call customer service at (815) 734-1104.